A BASIC CATHOLIC DICTIONARY

Daniel L. Lowery, C.SS.R.

LIGUORI
PUBLICATIONS

One Liguori Drive
Liguori, Missouri 63057
(314) 464-2500

Imprimi Potest:
John F. Dowd, C.SS.R.
Provincial, St. Louis Province
The Redemptorists

Imprimatur:
+ Edward J. O'Donnell
Vicar General, Archdiocese of St. Louis

ISBN 0-89243-241-1
Library of Congress Catalog Card Number: 85-80600
Printed in U.S.A.

In memory of my parents,
James Michael Lowery and
Josephine McCarthy Lowery,
my first and best teachers
in the ways of faith.

FOREWORD

Almost every Catholic experiences, at times, the need or desire to "look up" some point of Catholic doctrine, some liturgical celebration, some moral question, some outstanding name in the history of the Church. To provide such material, there are, to be sure, many resources available in most libraries (for example, the magnificent *New Catholic Encyclopedia,* comprising 18 large volumes!). Often enough, however, a person does not get around to visiting a library to follow up on a particular question. Gradually, then, the question fades from memory, and a good opportunity for refreshing one's religious knowledge passes by. At such times, a concise Catholic dictionary, available in one's home, would certainly come in handy!

To fill such a need, Liguori Publications herewith presents *A Basic Catholic Dictionary.* A few words about this title will throw light on the nature and purpose of the book itself.

First, it is a dictionary. One meaning of this term is: "a reference book listing alphabetically terms or names important to a particular subject or activity along with discussion of their meanings and applications" (*Webster's Seventh New Collegiate Dictionary*). *A Basic Catholic Dictionary* lists in alphabetical order some 450 terms and names, and provides a definition, description, or explanation of each.

Second, it is Catholic. That is to say, "the particular subject" treated in these pages is the Catholic Church: some of its beliefs, liturgical celebrations, outstanding personalities, moral teachings, and the like. In addition, I have also included some terms or names which, though not specifically Catholic, are of special interest to many Catholics.

Third, it is basic. My desire to keep this book compact and reasonably priced demanded that I make many choices. Of the innumerable topics that could have been included, I have chosen those which — on the basis of my pastoral experience of thirty years — seem to me to be of special importance and interest for the average Catholic.

This dictionary could not have reached the light of day without the help of many colleagues and friends. I am especially grateful to the entire editorial staff of Liguori Publications for many helpful suggestions. From the very beginning of this project until its completion I received a great deal of cooperation and encouragement from these talented people. I owe a special debt of thanks to John Bettin, Sue Anne Cole, O.S.U., and Patrick Kaler, C.SS.R., for reading the manuscript and offering many valuable suggestions, and to Christopher Farrell, C.SS.R., for his expert editing.

While I happily thank all of the above for their many suggestions and corrections, I must also acknowledge that I alone am responsible for the finished product and, therefore, for any lack of accuracy or clarity that may mar its pages.

My hope is that this book will find its way into many Catholic homes and that it will be of genuine service to those who use it. I would certainly be pleased to hear from those who make use of this dictionary, letting me know what strong and weak points they may have discovered. With this information, I would try to improve future editions so as to make this dictionary even more helpful and useful for Catholic readers of our day.

Daniel L. Lowery, C.SS.R.

A

ABBESS

The female superior of a monastic community of nuns (for example, Benedictines), elected by the community and having general religious authority over the community.

ABBOTT

The male superior of a monastic community of monks (for example, Benedictines), elected by the community and having general authority and ordinary jurisdiction over the community.

ABORTION

As understood here, the deliberate, intentional destruction of the human fetus at any stage after conception or the expulsion of it from the womb when it is not viable. It involves serious moral, legal, social, and canonical questions.

Morally, both from the viewpoint of natural law ethics and from divine revelation, abortion is a fundamental evil. The right to life is the most basic of all human rights; the right to life of the innocent is inviolable. The destruction of innocent human life is contrary to the law of God and is, in the words of the American Catholic bishops, "an unspeakable crime, a crime which subordinates weaker members of the human community to the interests of the stronger" (*To Live in Christ Jesus*).

Legally, the right to life of the unborn has traditionally been fully protected by law in civilized societies. In 1973, however, the Supreme Court of the United States rendered a decision legalizing abortion and, therefore, denying legal protection to the most helpless of innocent human beings. It is the conviction of many American citizens, including the majority of Catholics, that the Supreme Court's decision was morally and legally wrong and should be reversed.

Socially, this decision has brought about the formation of many pro-life groups who have as their purpose to inform and to educate American citizens on the basic issues at stake, to bring about a reversal of the Supreme Court's decision and so to insure legal protection for the unborn, and to address the specific needs of women with problems related to pregnancy so that they will have a realistic alternative to abortion.

According to Canon Law, a Catholic who actually procures an abortion incurs automatic excommunication (Canon 1398); accomplices (that is, those without whose assistance the abortion would not have been committed) also incur excommunication. See EXCOMMUNICATION.

ABRAHAM

One of the most extraordinary persons described in the Bible. His fascinating story is told especially in the Book of Genesis, chapters 12-25. Born in the nineteenth century before Christ, he was originally named Abram. When he was ninety-nine years old, the Lord appeared to him and said: "Between you and me I will establish my covenant, and I will multiply you exceedingly. . . . No longer shall you be called Abram; your name shall be Abraham, for I am making you the father of a host of nations" (Genesis 17:2-5). Because of his special calling, he is known as the father of the Jewish people and, by extension, the spiritual father of all believers. (The Church, in the third Eucharistic Prayer, refers to him as "our father in faith.") Faith, especially in the sense of absolute trust in God and fidelity to his will, was indeed his outstanding characteristic.

ABSOLUTION (SACRAMENTAL)

In the sacrament of Penance the absolution is the form (words) spoken by an authorized priest for the forgiveness of sins. The Church teaches that "Through the sign of absolution God grants pardon to the sinner who in sacramental confession manifests his change of heart to the Church's minister, and thus the sacrament of penance is completed" (*Rite of Penance,* 6d). See PENANCE, SACRAMENT OF.

ABSTINENCE

As understood in Catholic teaching, abstinence is a penitential practice of doing without (abstaining from) meat or another food or drink. According to the Code of Canon Law, "Abstinence from eating meat or another food according to the prescriptions of the conference of bishops is to be observed on Fridays throughout the year unless they are solemnities" and also on Ash Wednesday and Good Friday (Canon 1251). The conference of Catholic bishops is also empowered "to determine more precisely the observance of fast and abstinence and to substitute in whole or in part for fast and abstinence other forms of penance, especially works of charity and exercises of piety" (Canon 1253). The American Catholic bishops have determined that abstinence from meat is specifically required only on the Fridays of Lent (as well as on Ash Wednesday), but that some penance should be performed on each Friday of the year.

ACTS OF THE APOSTLES
One of the books of the New Testament, written by the evangelist Luke about A.D. 70 to 75. It describes the faith and way of life of the early Christians and the origin and spread of the Christian communities in New Testament times. It is a kind of history of the early Church (from about A.D. 30 to A.D. 67), but the author is not as much concerned with historical details as he is with the action of God in history. He describes the Church both as a mystery of God introduced into human history, especially through the preaching of the apostles, and also as a human organism compelled to adapt itself to actual circumstances in order to carry its mission to other places and cultures.

ADAM
According to the Book of Genesis, Adam is the father of the human race, the first man created by God (Genesis 1 and 2). He was expelled from the Garden of Eden because he disobeyed God's command not to eat of a certain tree. The Christian doctrine of original sin is traced back to Adam: through him the entire human race fell away from God's plan. In the New Testament, Jesus is described as the "new" or "second" Adam, bringing salvation to the human race. (See Romans 5 and 8.)

ADORATION
A conscious act of an intelligent creature by which God alone is recognized as worthy of supreme honor because of his infinite perfection and supreme dominion over creation. It is essentially

9

an act of the mind and will, but is commonly expressed in external acts of sacrifice, prayer, and reverence. Adoration in the strict sense is due to God alone.

ADULTERY

A voluntary act of sexual intercourse between a married person and another who is not that person's wife or husband. It is forbidden by the sixth commandment of the Decalogue ("You shall not commit adultery") and condemned as immoral in the New Testament (see Matthew 5:27 and Mark 10:19). Under the concept of adultery Jesus also included lustful desires (Matthew 5:27).

ADVENT

The season which opens the liturgical year of the Church. It begins on the fourth Sunday before Christmas and ends before the first Evening Prayer of Christmas. The liturgical readings and prayers place emphasis on the coming (advent, arrival) of Jesus Christ. The first part of Advent highlights his Second Coming at the end of time, and the second part (notably December 17-24) his coming into human history at the time of his birth in Bethlehem. This liturgical season features joy, hope, repentance, expectation, and preparation for the coming of Christ.

ADVENT WREATH

A wreath of laurel, spruce, holly, or similar foliage with four candles which are lighted successively in the weeks of Advent to symbolize the coming of Christ, the Light of the world. The lighting of the candles is usually accompanied by an appropriate hymn, a reading from Scripture, and/or prayers. Of German origin, the Advent wreath is now popular in American churches, schools, and homes.

ALB

See VESTMENTS.

ALLELUIA

A word of Hebrew origin meaning "praise Yahweh," it is used frequently in the liturgy, especially during the Easter season and at the "Alleluia verse" which precedes the reading of the Gospel at the Eucharistic liturgy. See YAHWEH.

ALL SAINTS

A liturgical solemnity celebrated on November 1. This feast commemorates all the blessed in heaven, but is especially designed to honor the blessed who have not been canonized and who have no special feast day. All Saints is a holy day of obligation on which Catholics are bound to participate in the Mass. See HOLY DAYS OF OBLIGATION.

ALL SOULS

A feast commemorating all the faithful departed, observed each year on November 2 (or, if November 2 is a Sunday, on November 3). Special prayers for the dead are offered on this day, a tradition which has come down to us from the earliest days of the Church. Pope Benedict XV granted each priest the privilege of celebrating three Masses on this day. A plenary indulgence for the souls in purgatory may be obtained on this day. See INDULGENCE; see PURGATORY.

ALPHONSUS LIGUORI, SAINT

Born near Naples, 1696, he was trained in law and practiced at the bar for eight years. Ordained a diocesan priest in 1726, he had great pastoral concern for the unevangelized poor in the country places outside the city. Founded the Congregation of the Most Holy Redeemer (Redemptorists) in 1732, especially to preach the Gospel to these poor people. He wrote over 100 books on the Christian life; is perhaps best known for his monumental four-volume work in moral theology for the guidance of confessors. His writings were instrumental in opposing the heresy of Jansenism. He was ordained a bishop in 1762 and served the diocese of St. Agatha of the Goths until 1775. He died in 1787, was canonized in 1839, declared a Doctor of the Church in 1871, and named the patron of confessors and moralists in 1950. See JANSENISM.

ALTAR

A table on which the Eucharistic sacrifice is celebrated. According to the Code of Canon Law, an altar may be fixed or movable; it is "*fixed* if it is so constructed that it is joined to the floor and therefore cannot be moved; it is *movable* if it can be transferred" (Canon 1235, §1). "According to church custom the table of a fixed altar is to be of stone, in fact of a single natural stone; nevertheless, even another material, worthy and solid, in the judgment of the conference of bishops also can be used. . . . A movable altar can be constructed from any solid material appropriate for liturgical use'' (Canon 1236, §1 and §2). Moreover, ''the ancient tradition of keeping the relics of martyrs and other saints under a fixed altar is to be preserved according to the norms given in the liturgical books'' (Canon 1237, §2).

AMEN

A Hebrew word meaning ''truly'' or ''so be it,'' it was used in the Jewish synagogue as a personal agreement with a prayer offered in the name of the community. In apostolic times it was taken over by the Christian community for scriptural and liturgical use. It is commonly used by Catholics at the end of liturgical prayers and as an affirmation of faith in receiving the Eucharist.

ANGEL

From the Greek word for messenger, the Bible speaks often of the role of angels. There are many Old Testament references to them (see, for example, Genesis 32:2; Isaiah 6; Daniel 10:13; Tobit 7:8). Of special note is the teaching of Jesus that angels are spiritual beings (Matthew 22:30), always enjoy the vision of God in heaven (Matthew 18:10), and will accompany him at his Second Coming (Matthew 16:27). In the course of centuries, theologians have described angels as created spirits without bodies, endowed with intellect and free will, inferior to God but superior to human beings. The Catholic Church professes that angels exist, but does not define any details about them.

ANGER

One of the capital or ''deadly'' sins, it is a feeling of displeasure, usually accompanied by antagonism, aroused by real or imaginary injury; it is sinful when accompanied by a deliberate desire for unjust retaliation. See CAPITAL SINS.

ANGLICANS

A word describing the churches united in faith and ecclesial organization to the English See of Canterbury. Originated in 1534 with Henry VIII's Act of Supremacy, declaring that the king should be the supreme head of the Church of England. (Note that in America Anglicans have been called Episcopalians since the Revolutionary War.) The absolute break with the Catholic Church occurred in 1563, when Parliament made the so-called Thirty-nine Articles of Religion mandatory for all citizens. Among the articles: the Bible contains all that is necessary for salvation; ecumenical councils are not infallible; transubstantiation is not acceptable (though today some Anglicans hold views on the Eucharist similar to those of the Catholic Church); the civil ruler has authority over the Church. The Book of Common Prayer is perhaps the most important bond of unity among Anglican churches.

ANNULMENT

A popular term for what is known in Canon Law as a decree of nullity — namely, a declaration by a competent authority of the Church that a marriage was invalid from the beginning because of the presence of a diriment (invalidating) impediment, a basic defect in consent to marriage or an inability to fulfill the responsibilities of marriage, or a condition placed by one or both of the partners on the very nature of marriage as understood by the Church. The annulment procedure may be started at the parish level; the investigation of the facts is usually carried out by the marriage tribunal under the leadership of the bishop. See IMPEDIMENTS TO MARRIAGE.

ANNUNCIATION

A liturgical solemnity, celebrated on March 25, which commemorates the angel Gabriel's announcement of the Incarnation of the Son of God to the Virgin Mary. (See Luke 1:26-38.) The origin of this feast goes back to at least the fifth century.

ANOINTING OF THE SICK, SACRAMENT OF

One of the seven sacraments of the Church, described thus in the new Code of Canon Law: "The anointing of the sick by which the Church commends to the suffering and glorified Lord the faithful who are dangerously sick so that He relieve and save them, is conferred by anointing them with oil and using the words prescribed in the liturgical books" (Canon 998). This sacrament can be administered only by a bishop or priest. It is properly "administered to a member of the faithful who, after having reached the use of reason, begins to be in danger due to sickness or old age" (Canon 1004, §1).

ANTICHRIST

A term used to describe the chief of Christ's enemies. The term is used in the New Testament only, in 1 John 2:18,24, 4:3; and 2 John 7. Historically, the Antichrist has been identified with individual persons (that is, Caligula, Hitler) or with social institutions. Some non-Catholics preach that the Catholic Church is the Antichrist. We have no definite identification of the Antichrist from the Bible or from the Church, but a common opinion of Catholic theologians is that the reference is to a real person.

ANTIPOPE

One who claimed to be pope in opposition to the validly elected pope. Some thirty of these have existed in the history of the Church, the last in the fifteenth century.

APOSTLE

From a Greek word meaning "one who is sent," this term is used often in the New Testament. It is specifically used to describe the Twelve whom Jesus gathered around him for special instruction and the eleven of them chosen as prime witnesses to the Resurrection and for leadership roles in the Christian community. According to Catholic teaching, Christ ordained them priests at the Last Supper and commissioned them to preach the Gospel to all humankind (see Matthew 28:19-20).

APOSTLES' CREED

A summary of Christian faith expressed in twelve articles. Its name came from a popular belief that it was actually written by the Twelve Apostles; its substance clearly stems from the New Testament. Historians, however, date the actual text anywhere from A.D. 150 to A.D. 400. It is clear that at a very early date the Western Church required catechumens (new members) to learn the Apostles' Creed before Baptism. It is still considered an excellent summary of the Christian faith.

APOSTOLIC SUCCESSION

A term that affirms the uninterrupted handing on of episcopal power and authority from the apostles to contemporary bishops. This successive transfer is effected whenever a validly ordained bishop ordains a successor by the laying on of hands. Those ordained as bishops have continued to fulfill the roles of the apostles, and have been continually in communion with the Apostolic See, that is, with the Bishop of Rome.

ASCENSION OF THE LORD
The rising of Christ to heaven after his Resurrection, witnessed by the apostles and referred to frequently in the New Testament (see, for example, Mark 16:19; Luke 24:51; Acts 1:9). His return marked the exaltation of Christ to the right hand of the Father, where he now exercises all power in heaven and on earth (see, for example, John 14:2; Philippians 3:21). Ascension Thursday (kept on the sixth Thursday after Easter) is one of the principal feast days of the Christian year and is for Catholics a holy day of obligation.

ASSUMPTION OF MARY
A truth of faith, proclaimed as a dogma by Pope Pius XII on November 1, 1950, which holds that "the Immaculate Mother of God, the ever-Virgin Mary, having completed the course of her earthly life, was assumed body and soul into heavenly glory." This belief of the Church was evident from the very early days of the Church. The feast of Mary's Assumption, celebrated on August 15, is one of the principal Marian feasts of the Church year and is for Catholics a holy day of obligation.

ATHEISM
A denial of the existence of God. A distinction is often made between intellectual atheism (that is, a system of thought which asserts that the existence of God is contrary to fact or reason) and practical atheism (that is, that human acts have no relationship to God). There are innumerable variations of atheism, a number of which are described in Vatican II's The Church in the Modern World, #19-21.

AUGUSTINE, SAINT
Born in Tagaste, North Africa, in A.D. 354, of a pagan father and a Christian mother (Saint Monica). He was educated somewhat

in the Christian faith but soon lost it as he became involved in many of the philosophical currents of his time. After a number of years spent searching for the meaning of life and living in a pagan way, he was converted and baptized in 387. He later became the Bishop of Hippo and is considered one of the most influential Fathers of the Church because of his penetrating explanations of Christian truth. He wrote many books on Christian faith and life, including the well-known *Confessions* and *The City of God*. He died in A.D. 430. See FATHERS OF THE CHURCH.

AVARICE

One of the capital or "deadly" sins, it is an excessive love for material things to the neglect of spiritual goods and one's obligations of justice and charity.

B

BAPTISM, SACRAMENT OF

The first of the seven sacraments, described by the Church in this way: "Baptism, the gate to the sacraments, necessary for salvation in fact or at least in intention, by which men and women are freed from their sins, are reborn as children of God and, configured to Christ by an indelible character, are incorporated in the Church, is validly conferred only by washing with true water together with the required form of words" (Canon 849).

The following points of Church law should be noted: (*a*) Baptism may be conferred either by immersion or by pouring; (*b*) the water used in Baptism should be blessed, but in case of necessity unblessed water is licit; (*c*) the required form of words is, "I baptize you in the name of the Father, and of the Son, and of the Holy Spirit"; (*d*) it is recommended that Baptism be celebrated on a Sunday or if possible at the Easter Vigil; (*e*) the proper place for Baptism is a church or oratory, but in case of necessity it may be conferred in a private home or in a hospital; (*f*) the ordinary minister of Baptism is a bishop, priest, or deacon, but others may be deputed for this function (as often happens in mission territories) and in case of necessity any person can and should confer Baptism.

BAPTISMAL CANDLE

In the Catholic rite of Baptism there is a section called the "presentation of the lighted candle." A smaller candle is lit from the Easter candle, symbol of Christ as Light of the world, and presented to an adult being baptized or, in the case of an infant, to the father (or, in his absence, the sponsor) of the child, with the admonition to "walk always as a child of the light and keep the flame of faith alive in your heart."

BAPTISMAL FONT

A container for holding the baptismal water; it is usually made of durable material and properly ornamented. Every parish church is to have a baptismal font. In recent years the baptismal font has been given a prominent and visible place in the church building. See BAPTISTERY.

BAPTISMAL NAME

The name given to the person at Baptism; according to a long Christian tradition, this name should be that of one of the saints so that the baptized person will have a special heavenly patron and will be encouraged to imitate the life and holiness of the saint. The present law of the Church expresses this tradition in a negative way: "Parents, sponsors and the pastor are to see to it that a name foreign to a Christian mentality is not given" (Canon 855).

BAPTISMAL PREPARATION

A period of preparation before Baptism. An adult who wishes to be baptized must first "be sufficiently instructed in the truths of faith and in Christian obligations and be tested in the Christian life by means of the catechumenate" (Canon 865). Before the Baptism of an infant, the parents (or at least one parent) must give consent to the Baptism and must give assurance that they understand the importance of Baptism and that the infant will be brought up in the Catholic religion. If such assurance is lacking, the Baptism is to be delayed with the hope that the parents will become more aware of their religious responsibilities. See CATECHUMENATE.

BAPTISMAL REGISTER

The record of the Baptism to be completed by the priest or deacon who performs the Baptism and kept in the archives of the parish. A copy of this record is usually given to the baptized at the time of the Baptism and is available on request.

BAPTISMAL ROBE

In the Catholic rite of Baptism there is a section called the "clothing with the white garment"; at this time the person being baptized is symbolically covered with a white garment and exhorted to "bring it unstained to the judgment seat of our Lord Jesus Christ so that you may have everlasting life."

BAPTISMAL SPONSORS

Popularly known as godparents, sponsors play an important part in Baptism. Canons 872-874 give the following norms in reference to baptismal sponsors or godparents: (a) "Insofar as possible one to be baptized is to be given a sponsor who is to assist an adult in Christian initiation, or, together with the parents, to present an infant at the baptism, and who will help the baptized to lead a Christian life in harmony with baptism, and to fulfill faithfully the obligations connected with it"; (b) "Only one male or one female or one of each sex is to be employed"; (c) "To be admitted to the role of sponsor, a person must: (1) be designated by the one to be baptized, by the parents or the one who takes their place or, in their absence, by the pastor or minister and is to have the qualifications and intentions of performing this role; (2) have completed the sixteenth year, unless a different age has been established by the diocesan bishop or it seems to the pastor or minister that an exception is to be made for a just cause; (3) be a Catholic who has been confirmed and has already received the sacrament of the Most Holy Eucharist and leads a life in harmony with the faith and the role to be undertaken; (4) not be bound by any canonical penalty legitimately imposed or declared; (5) not be the father or the mother of the one to be baptized." Finally, it should be noted that a non-Catholic may not be a baptismal sponsor for a Catholic, but may serve as a witness to the Baptism together with a Catholic sponsor.

BAPTISMAL VOWS

The renunciation of Satan and all his works and the profession of faith by the one to be baptized or, in the case of an infant, by the parents and sponsor. The solemn renewal of these vows is part of the Easter Vigil. The private renewal of these vows is a commendable act of piety.

BAPTISM OF BLOOD

Also called Baptism of martyrdom, this term refers to the case of a person who freely and patiently suffered death for the Christian faith before he or she could actually receive the sacrament of

Baptism — not an uncommon occurrence, especially in the first three centuries of Christianity and in other times of persecution.

BAPTISM OF DESIRE
This term refers to the state of those who, in the words of Vatican II, "through no fault of their own, do not know the gospel of Christ or His Church, yet sincerely seek God and, moved by grace, strive by their deeds to do His will as it is known to them through the dictates of conscience . . ." (Dogmatic Constitution on the Church, #16).

BAPTISM OF INFANTS
The teaching of the Catholic Church on the Baptism of infants is this: "From the earliest times, the Church, to which the mission of preaching the gospel and of baptizing was entrusted, has baptized infants as well as adults. Our Lord said: 'Unless a man is reborn in water and the Holy Spirit, he cannot enter the kingdom of God.' The Church has always understood these words to mean that children should not be deprived of baptism, because they are baptized in the faith of the Church. This faith is proclaimed for them by their parents and godparents, who represent both the local Church and the whole society of saints and believers. . . . To fulfill the true meaning of the sacrament, children must later be formed in the faith in which they have been baptized . . . so that they may ultimately accept for themselves the faith in which they have been baptized" (Rite of Baptism for Children, 2-3). The present law of the Church obliges parents to "see to it that infants are baptized within the first weeks after birth"; in danger of death, an infant is to be baptized "without any delay" (Canon 867, §1 and §2).

BAPTISTERY
A section of a church, or even a separate room or building, which contains the baptismal font and is set aside for the celebration of Baptism. Commonly found near the main entrance of the church, it is considered a structure of great importance in the church building.

BAPTISTS
The largest Protestant denomination in the world, it originated in Europe in the seventeenth century, with strong roots in Cal-

vinism. Roger Williams founded the first Baptist church in the United States in Rhode Island. A wide variety of theological views is found among Baptists, and there are a large number of separate groups bearing the name. In a most general way, however, it can be said that Baptists agree that the Bible is the sole rule of faith, that the adult believer should be baptized by total immersion, that infants should not be baptized, that all the faithful share in the priesthood, that the local church should be independent, and Church and State should be separated. The Baptists in the United States have a strong commitment to evangelization and to overseas missions.

BASIL, SAINT

Born in A.D. 329, he dedicated himself to the monastic life for many years. In 370 he became the Bishop of Caesarea and strongly defended the teaching of the Church against the heresy of Arianism, which denied the divinity of Christ; between 358 and 364 he produced a monastic rule which is still in use. Today he is known as "the father of Eastern monasticism." He died in 379.

BEATIFICATION

A declaration by the pope that a deceased person lived a holy life and is now in heaven and is worthy of public veneration on a limited (not universal) basis in the Church. This act usually follows upon a process by which the life, virtue, reputation for holiness, ministry, and writings of the person are intensely scrutinized by the Church. Those who are beatified are called "Blessed."

BEATITUDES

The promises of Christ concerning happiness or blessedness as proclaimed in the Sermon on the Mount. In the Gospel of Matthew (5:3-11) eight are listed; in the Gospel of Luke (6:20-22) four are stated. They are considered basic qualities of Christian holiness which will be generously rewarded by God.

BENEDICT, SAINT

Born in A.D. 480 he became a hermit at about the age of twenty and lived this way of life for some years. He founded a series of monasteries, beginning at Subiaco, Italy; around 525 he founded the monastery at Monte Cassino and there developed his highly acclaimed monastic rule; he is known as "the father of Western monasticism"; his rule is still used not only by his own religious order (men and women known as Benedictines) but also by some other religious orders. Benedictine monasteries (with the famous motto *Ora et Labora,* that is, "Pray and Work") exist in almost every nation of the world. Saint Benedict's sister was Saint Scholastica. Benedict died circa 546.

BENEDICTION OF THE BLESSED SACRAMENT
A Eucharistic devotion approved by the Church for certain occasions and under certain conditions; it consists in the benediction (blessing) of the people with the sacred Host (usually contained in a monstrance); the blessing is to be preceded by readings from the word of God, hymns, prayers, and a suitable time for silent adoration. Its purpose is to highlight the marvelous presence of Christ in the Eucharist. See MONSTRANCE.

BIBLE
Also called Sacred Scripture or the Scriptures, the Bible is a collection of books accepted by the Church as the inspired, authentic account of God's revelation about himself and his plan of salvation for the human race. The Bible is divided into the Old Testament and the New Testament. The Old Testament contains 46 books, written in Hebrew between the years 900 B.C. and 160 B.C. Included are books with distinct purposes: historical, moral, prophetic. These books are a record of Yahweh God's dealing with the Israelites, "the Chosen People," and of their response to him and his plan. The New Testament contains 27 books, written in Greek between the years A.D. 50 and A.D. 140. Included are the four Gospels of Matthew, Mark, Luke, and John, the Acts of the Apostles, the Epistles (Letters) of Saint Paul, other Epistles, and the Book of Revelation. The major theme of the New Testament is Jesus Christ: his person, his preaching, his saving death and Resurrection, and his relationship to us as Lord and Savior.

BIRTH CONTROL
A popular, less technical term for contraception. See CONTRACEPTION; see NATURAL FAMILY PLANNING.

BISHOP

According to the Code of Canon Law, "Through the Holy Spirit who has been given to them, bishops are the successors of the apostles by divine institution; they are constituted pastors within the Church so that they are teachers of doctrine, priests of sacred worship and ministers of governance" and "By the fact of their episcopal consecration bishops receive along with the function of sanctifying also the functions of teaching and of ruling, which by their very nature, however, can be exercised only when they are in hierarchical communion with the head of the college and its members" (Canon 375, §1 and §2). Bishops are empowered to ordain priests and deacons and other bishops.

BLASPHEMY

Speaking or acting against God (or persons or objects consecrated to God) in a contemptuous or irreverent way; a serious violation of the reverence and love due to God.

BLESSED SACRAMENT

See EUCHARIST.

BLESSING

Placing a person or object under the care of God or dedicating a person or thing to the service of God. A simple blessing is usually made with the sign of the cross, sometimes accompanied by sprinkling holy water. The Church also has a large number of specific blessings for various times and occasions. See SACRAMENTALS; see SIGN OF THE CROSS.

BODY

An essential part of the human person, the body is a fundamentally good creation of God; according to Catholic teaching, the body is a temple of God and therefore deserving of respect by oneself and others.

BODY, RESURRECTION OF

According to Scripture and the formal teaching of the Catholic Church, the body will be resurrected and reunited to the soul after death. Christ taught the resurrection of the body (see Matthew

22:29-32; Luke 14:14; John 5:29). The doctrine was preached as a fundamental mystery of Christian faith (1 Corinthians 15:20; Revelation 20:12) and was included in all of the early creeds.

BREVIARY

The book or books containing the official and public prayer of the Church known as the Liturgy of the Hours (also called Divine Office): that is, a set form of prayers, hymns, and readings designed to sanctify the various hours of the day; at present, the breviary contains the office of readings, morning prayer, day-time prayer, evening prayer, and night prayer. Men in Holy Orders and men and women in solemn vows are required by Church law to pray the Liturgy of the Hours; all other members of the Church are strongly encouraged to do the same.

BUDDHISM

The religious thought and practice of Siddhartha Gautama, born in 563 B.C., known as the Buddha or Enlightened One, who in meditation was enlightened as to the passing nature of the visible world and concluded that suffering is universal in this passing world, that suffering comes from desire, and therefore the extinction or suppression of desire will cause suffering to cease. The Buddhist Way of Perfection teaches how desire can be suppressed by following an eightfold path: right understanding, right purpose, right speech, right conduct, right work, right effort, right mindfulness, right contemplation. Buddhism (including the more modern versions) is still one of the largest religions of the world, especially in the Orient. Buddha died around 483 B.C.

BURIAL, ECCLESIASTICAL

The interment of a deceased person in consecrated or blessed ground after the funeral rites in which ''the Church asks spiritual assistance for the departed, honors their bodies, and at the same time brings the solace of hope to the living'' (Canon 1176, §2); Church law (Canon 1184) forbids ecclesiastical burial for certain persons, such as notorious apostates or public sinners, who have not given some signs of repentance. See CREMATION.

BYZANTINE RITE

The official ritual practice of the Church of Constantinople (formerly Byzantium) which also has its own general law; after the Roman Rite, it is the most widely used of the rites, practiced both by many Eastern Orthodox Christians and also by Catholics of the Byzantine Rite (that is, those who are in union with the pope of Rome). See EASTERN CHURCHES, CATHOLIC; EASTERN CHURCHES, SEPARATED.

C

CALUMNY

Also referred to as "slander," calumny is one of the ways in which one person can injure or ruin the reputation of another; it is injuring or ruining the reputation of another by lies, and is a violation of charity, justice, and truth.

CANONIZATION

The declaration by the pope that a person is a saint, is now in heaven, and is worthy of veneration by all of the faithful. This declaration is usually preceded by the process of beatification and by a detailed examination of the person's life and writings; two miracles ascribed to his or her intercession must ordinarily be authenticated by the Church before the declaration is made. See BEATIFICATION.

CANON LAW

The official body of laws for Catholics of the Roman or Latin Rite, contained in one volume called the *Code of Canon Law*. (Note that Eastern Rite Christians in union with Rome have their own laws which are at present being codified.) The first Code of Canon Law for the Roman Church, containing 2,414 canons (laws) on all aspects of the Church's life, was promulgated in 1917; the revised Code, containing 1,752 canons, was promulgated in 1983. It contains laws that apply to all members of the Church, others that define and govern the hierarchy of the Church and members of religious communities; there are norms governing the teaching office and the sanctifying office of the Church, including a long section on the sacraments. The Code of Canon Law, in the words of Pope John Paul II, "is in no way intended as a substitute for faith, grace, charisms, and especially charity in the life of the Church and of the faithful. On the contrary, its purpose is rather to create such an order in the ecclesial society that, while assigning the primacy to love, grace and charisms, it at the same time renders their organic development easier in the life of both the ecclesial society and the individual persons who belong to it.''

CANON OF THE MASS
A term referring to the Eucharistic Prayer of the Mass and containing the solemn and essential act of consecration in which the species of bread and wine are changed into the Body and Blood of Jesus Christ and the sacrifice of Christ on the Cross is perpetuated over the centuries. The prayers of the Canon recall the great mysteries of the Christian faith and include prayers for the Church, for the living and the dead, and remembrances of the saints and martyrs. As of 1985, the Church has approved four Eucharistic Prayers for general use, three for Masses with children, and two for Masses of reconciliation.

CANON OF THE SCRIPTURE
The list or collection of books of the Bible officially recognized and accepted by the Church as the inspired word of God and therefore to be taken as the rule or norm of faith.

CAPITAL PUNISHMENT
A form of punishment whereby the state takes the life of the person proven guilty of serious crimes. The morality of the death penalty has been debated for centuries. In general, Catholic teaching has accepted in principle that the state has the right to take the life of a person proven guilty of serious crimes. But there continues to be a serious debate about whether capital punishment is justified in practice, that is, in the concrete circumstances of modern life. In recent years Pope John Paul II and the American Catholic bishops have strongly opposed the actual use of capital punishment and have called for its practical abolition.

CAPITAL SINS
Popularly, often referred to as "the deadly sins," they are the chief sinful tendencies of fallen human nature, the main sources

from which other particular sins arise; traditionally, they are pride, avarice, lust, envy, gluttony, anger, and sloth.

CATECHESIS
Instruction and formation in the Catholic faith, both for those who are preparing to be baptized and for those who are already baptized but in need of continuing instruction and formation according to their age and their level of maturity in the Christian life.

CATECHISM
A summary or manual containing the basics of Christian doctrine, usually in question-and-answer form.

CATECHUMENATE
The period of instruction and involvement in the Catholic faith in preparation for the Baptism of adults or for the reception of baptized non-Catholic Christians into the Catholic Church; the basic elements of the catechumenate are explained in the Rite of Christian Initiation of Adults (RCIA).

CATHOLIC
From a Greek word meaning "universal," it is part of the official title or designation given to the body of Christian communities in union with the Bishop of Rome (the pope); it was used to describe the Church by Saint Ignatius of Antioch in approximately A.D. 107: "Wherever the Bishop shall appear, there let the people be, even as where Jesus is, there is the Catholic Church." The word is now used in a variety of ways: for example, to describe the universality of the Church itself as intended for all human beings; to identify particular institutions of the Church (for example, "the Catholic Press") and individual members of the Church (for example, "John Doe is a good Catholic").

CELIBACY
In general, the unmarried state of life; in Christian teaching, celibacy is a vocation in which one freely chooses to be unmarried "for the sake of God's reign" (Matthew 19:11), a vocation that may be lived in the lay state or in a religious institute publicly recognized by the Church; according to the Code of

Canon Law for the Latin Rite, celibacy is required of candidates for the priesthood. See CHASTITY.

CHALICE

The cup containing the wine which in the Eucharistic sacrifice is changed into the precious Blood of Christ. It must be constructed of appropriate materials and should be blessed by a bishop or priest.

CHANCERY

The administrative office of the diocese where the ordinary business of the diocese is conducted, records kept, meetings held, and the like.

CHARISM

Extraordinary gifts or graces of the Holy Spirit given to individuals for the sake of others. Saint Paul lists nine of these graces (1 Corinthians 12:4-11); he also insists that the virtue of charity is above all other charisms (1 Corinthians 13).

CHARISMATIC MOVEMENT

Also known as the Catholic Pentecostal Movement, this is a relatively recent movement in the Catholic Church, originating in 1967. This movement believes that there is a new outpouring of the Holy Spirit in the Catholic Church, a need to reawaken Catholics to the gifts of the Holy Spirit and to the baptism of the Holy Spirit, that is, a personal experience of the graces already sacramentally received. Generally, charismatic communities have weekly meetings consisting of Scripture readings and teachings, prayer, singing of hymns, sharing of experiences, and fellowship. The movement has attracted many Catholics (perhaps as many as six million) in the United States.

CHARITY

One of the theological (God-given and God-directed) virtues infused into the soul with sanctifying grace, providing the ability and inclination to love God above all things and to love others for the sake of God; it is the greatest of all the virtues. See SANCTIFYING GRACE.

CHASTITY

The virtue that moderates and regulates the sexual appetite according to the principles of right reason and the law of God; this virtue applies to all, both married and single, but is expressed differently according to one's state of life. This virtue, according to the Vatican's *Declaration on Sexual Ethics*, "increases the human person's dignity and enables him or her to love truly, disinterestedly, unselfishly and with respect for others" (#12).

The vow of chastity is one of the evangelical counsels (see Matthew 19:11) and one of the three vows (together with obedience and poverty) professed by religious in the Church. See RELIGIOUS.

CHRIST

A title of Jesus meaning the Anointed One, identical to the Hebrew word Messiah, that is, Savior or Deliverer. To acknowledge Jesus as the Christ is to acknowledge him as Savior.

CHRISTMAS

The feast of the Nativity of Jesus Christ, celebrated on December 25. The liturgy provides three different Masses for the feast (midnight, dawn, during the day), and priests are permitted to celebrate all three Christmas Masses. Many of the customs that have grown up over the centuries to celebrate Christmas had their origin in the pagan celebration of the beginning of winter but have been "christened" with a religious significance.

CHURCH

The Church may be defined as that visible religious society founded by Jesus Christ, under one head (Saint Peter and his successors), whose purpose is to preserve and proclaim his teachings and to make present his sacrifice and sacraments for the salvation of all until the end of time. The Church is known by the marks that characterize it: it is one, holy, catholic, and apostolic. Vatican II (in the Dogmatic Constitution on the Church) offered many images and descriptions to try to communicate the total meaning of the Church: it is the new People of God; it is the Mystical Body of Jesus Christ, "the whole Christ, head and members"; it is a sacrament or sign of God's presence;

it is a community of believers united with Christ, especially in and through the Eucharist; it is an assembly of the faithful, committed to carry forth the mission of Christ under the guidance of the Holy Spirit.

CIRCUMCISION

From a religious viewpoint, circumcision was very important to the people of Israel: it was a "mark of the covenant" between Yahweh and his people (see Genesis 17:10-14). Jesus himself was circumcised on the eighth day after his birth (Luke 2:21), and the early Christians were sometimes referred to as simply "the circumcised" (see Acts 11:2). It was soon recognized, however, that the Mosaic Law need not be imposed on Gentile Christians and that circumcision was no longer a religious requirement for the baptized. "In Christ Jesus neither circumcision nor the lack of it counts for anything; only faith, which expresses itself through love" (Galatians 5:6; see also Galatians 6:15 and Romans 3:30).

CLERGY

A title referring to those men who are ordained for the service of God and the Church, including deacons, priests, and bishops. A distinction may be made between diocesan clergy, that is, those ordained for a particular diocese and committed in obedience to a particular bishop; and regular (or religious) clergy, that is, those who belong to a religious institute in the Church and owe primary obedience to their religious superiors as well as pastoral obedience to the bishop in whose diocese they exercise their ministry.

COLLEGE OF CARDINALS

According to the Code of Canon Law, "The cardinals of the Holy Roman Church constitute a special college whose responsibility is to provide for the election of the Roman Pontiff in accord with the norm of special law; the cardinals assist the Roman Pontiff collegially when they are called together to deal with questions of major importance; they do so individually when they assist the Roman Pontiff especially in the daily care of the universal Church by means of the different offices which they perform" (Canon 349). Further details about the appointment and role of cardinals may be found in Canons 350 to 359.

COLLEGIALITY

In the strict sense, this term refers to the fact that all the bishops of the Church in union with and subordinate to the pope, the Bishop of Rome, possess supreme teaching and pastoral authority over the whole Church. This authority is exercised most clearly in ecumenical councils, but also in other ways sanctioned by the pope. Collegiality is considered an essential element of the Church as instituted by Christ; it is explained at length in Vatican II's Dogmatic Constitution on the Church.

In a wide sense, this term is often used to describe other forms of co-responsibility in various ecclesiastical communities, such as the diocese, the parish, or the religious community.

COMMANDMENTS OF GOD

A term often applied to the Decalogue or Ten Commandments as given by God to Moses on Mount Sinai (see Exodus 20:1-21 and Deuteronomy 5:2-33) and interpreted by Jesus Christ (see Matthew 5:17-48). As given in the Book of Exodus, the Ten Commandments are as follows:

I, the LORD, am your God. . . . You shall not have other gods besides me. . . .
You shall not take the name of the LORD, your God, in vain.
Remember to keep holy the sabbath day. . . .
Honor your father and your mother. . . .
You shall not kill.
You shall not commit adultery.
You shall not steal.
You shall not bear false witness against your neighbor.
You shall not covet your neighbor's house. . . .
You shall not covet your neighbor's wife. . . .

COMMANDMENTS OF THE CHURCH

See PRECEPTS OF THE CHURCH.

COMMUNION OF SAINTS

One of the articles of the Apostles' Creed is "I believe in . . . the communion of saints," a term which describes the spiritual bond that exists between all the members of the Church: the saints in

32

heaven, the souls in purgatory, and the faithful still living on earth. According to Catholic teaching, all are united with Christ and with one another in grace, prayer, and good works. See PURGATORY.

CONFESSION
See PENANCE, SACRAMENT OF.

CONFIRMATION, SACRAMENT OF
One of the seven sacraments described thus by the Church: "The sacrament of confirmation impresses a character and by it the baptized, continuing on the path of Christian initiation, are enriched by the gift of the Holy Spirit and bound more perfectly to the Church; it strengthens them and obliges them more firmly to be witnesses to Christ by word and deed and to spread and defend the faith" (Canon 879).

This sacrament is conferred through anointing with chrism on the forehead, which is done by the imposition of the hand, and through the words: "Be sealed with the Gift of the Holy Spirit." The ordinary minister of Confirmation is a bishop, though there are cases when a priest is authorized to confirm. The general norm of Canon Law is that this sacrament should be conferred "at about the age of discretion," but the conterence of bishops may determine another age. In the United States, most dioceses seem to favor an older age. The person to be confirmed should ordinarily be suitably instructed and prepared for this sacrament. As far as possible each person being confirmed should have a sponsor; the same norms apply to the sponsor at Confirmation as those governing the sponsor at Baptism; it is desirable that the person who was sponsor at one's Baptism be sponsor for one's Confirmation as well. See BAPTISMAL SPONSOR.

CONSCIENCE
A dictate of the practical reason or a personal judgment which decides, on the basis of general moral values and principles, that an act one is about to do is morally good or evil because it does or does not conform to God's law of love. Vatican II spoke of conscience in many ways: "In the depths of his conscience, man detects a law which he does not impose upon himself, but which holds him to obedience. Always summoning him to love good

and avoid evil, the voice of conscience can when necessary speak to his heart more specifically: do this, shun that. For man has in his heart a law written by God. To obey it is the very dignity of man; according to it he will be judged.

Conscience is the most secret core and sanctuary of a man. There he is alone with God, whose voice echoes in his depths. In a wonderful manner conscience reveals that law which is fulfilled by love of God and neighbor'' (Pastoral Constitution on the Church in the Modern World, #16).

CONTEMPLATION

A form of interior, affective prayer in which one admires or rests in the knowledge and love of God. In the words of Saint John of the Cross, "Contemplation is the science of love, which is an infused loving knowledge of God." In its purest form contemplation is a gift of the Holy Spirit. See QUIET, PRAYER OF.

CONTRACEPTION

The deliberate and positive interference with sexual intercourse in order to avoid conception. The constant teaching of the Church, even from earliest times, is that contraception is morally wrong. In modern times this teaching has been strongly restated by Pope Paul VI in his encyclical *Humanae Vitae* and by Pope John Paul II in a number of places. According to Pope Paul VI, "each and every marriage act must remain open to new life" and, as a consequence, "every action which, either in anticipation of the conjugal act, or in its accomplishment, or in the development of its natural consequences, proposes, whether as an end or a means, to render procreation impossible" must be excluded as a licit means of regulating births (*Humanae Vitae,* 14). See NATURAL FAMILY PLANNING.

CONTRITION

In the words of the Council of Trent, contrition is "heartfelt sorrow and aversion for the sin committed along with the intention of sinning no more." In the sacrament of Penance, contrition is the most important act of the penitent. A theological distinction may be made between perfect contrition and imperfect contrition (also called attrition). Perfect contrition is sorrow for sin arising out of the motive of love of God, while imperfect contrition is sorrow for sin arising out of some lesser motive, such as fear arising from the anticipated loss of heaven or condemnation to hell.

CONVERSION

In the New Testament the Greek word *metanoia,* often translated as conversion or repentance, means something very profound and personal: not merely a change of manners but a change of heart, a turning away from sin, a return to the Father's love. In the words of Pope Paul VI: ''We can only approach the kingdom of Christ by metanoia (conversion). This is a profound change of the whole person by which one begins to consider, judge, and arrange his or her life according to the holiness and love of God, made manifest in his Son in the last days and given to us in abundance.''

COVENANT

A word meaning a formal agreement, pact, or contract; in religious terms it describes the special relationship between God and his people. The Old Testament gives many examples of God's covenant with the Israelites: for example, with Abraham (see Genesis 15 and following), with Noah (see Genesis 6:18), with Moses (see Deuteronomy 5, 6, 7). In the covenant God promised to be faithful to his people; and they, in turn, promised to be faithful to him, to worship him alone, and to keep his commandments. One of the dominant themes of the Old Testament is that while God is always faithful to his part of the covenant, the Israelites are not always faithful to theirs. The New Testament describes the new covenant: that is the special relationship between God the Father, Jesus his beloved Son, and each Christian in and with Jesus. The new covenant does not annul the old but, in Jesus, brings it to fulfillment (see Galatians 3:15-29). In the new covenant Jesus expresses unconditional love for his people, instructs them, forgives them, and lays down his life for them, thus sealing the new covenant in his blood: ''This cup is the new covenant in my blood. Do this, whenever you drink it, in remembrance of me'' (1 Corinthians 11:25).

CREED

A summary of the principal truths of the Church in the form of a profession of faith. Two of the most important creeds are the

Apostles' Creed and the Nicene Creed. See APOSTLES' CREED; see NICENE CREED.

CREMATION
The disposal of the dead by reducing the body to ashes. The Church strongly condemned cremation in the past because the practice was associated with a denial of the Christian doctrine of the resurrection of the dead. The present teaching of the Church, as expressed in Canon Law, is as follows: "The Church earnestly recommends that the pious custom of burying the bodies of the dead be observed; it does not, however, forbid cremation unless it has been chosen for reasons which are contrary to Christian teaching" (Canon 1176, §3). See BURIAL, ECCLESIASTICAL.

CROSS
A term that describes the instrument of suffering on which Christ died for the salvation of the world; thus, the cross is a symbol of Christ's redeeming love, profoundly respected by Christians throughout the world. Also, a term that describes the suffering or mortification of a Christian, especially when accepted lovingly in union with the sufferings of Christ: "If a man wishes to come after me, he must deny his very self, take up his cross, and follow in my steps" (Mark 8:34).

CRUCIFIX
A cross bearing the image of Christ either as suffering Savior or as Risen Lord. A crucifix must be on or over the altar where Mass is celebrated. Among Catholics, a blessed crucifix is a revered object of private and public devotion.

CULTS
A term that in modern times refers to particular religious or semireligious groups noteworthy for esoteric beliefs, rituals, practices.

CURSILLO
An intense, three-day experience of Christian renewal involving community living, presentations on Christian doctrine by lay persons and priests, participation in group discussions, liturgical prayer, and the like. The Cursillo is followed by a post-Cursillo

program focusing on weekly meetings of small groups and larger reunions (called Ultreyas) in which participants share prayer and insights. The Cursillo movement originated in Spain in 1949; it was introduced in the United States in 1957. Since then it has been established in many dioceses throughout the nation.

D

DANIEL, BOOK OF

One of the books of the Old Testament, containing 14 chapters, written between 167 and 164 B.C., a time of persecution. The overall purpose of this book was to give comfort and reassurance to the Jewish people during the persecution. The Book of Daniel belongs to a type of literature known as "apocalyptic"; this literature emphasizes that Yahweh is the Lord of history, that he will ultimately vindicate his people, and that the kingdom of God will eventually be victorious against persecutors.

DAVID

The second, and perhaps the greatest, king of the Israelites, a major recipient of the messianic promises, David ascended the throne about 1000 B.C. after having been the armor-bearer of King Saul. (His engaging story is told especially in 1 Samuel 16 and following and 2 Samuel.) One of his greatest accomplishments was seizing the city of Jerusalem from the Jebusites, defeating the Philistines, and transforming the disparate tribes of Israel into an organized and united nation. He was a religious poet who wrote a number of the Psalms (though by no means all of them) and a religious man who desired to serve the Lord in obedience; his grave sins (adultery and murder) are described in the Bible, but so also is his repentance. The promises made to him and his descendants are fulfilled in Jesus. See PSALMS.

DEACON

A man who is ordained for service to the People of God. In apostolic times the ministry of deacon was to serve various corporal and spiritual needs of the community (Acts 6:1-7) and to assist in preaching the word of God (Acts 8:40). Because of his important ministry, the deacon was expected to be a man of religious and moral integrity (see 1 Timothy 3:8-11). In the

Church there are two kinds of deacons: those who receive the order as they advance to the priesthood and those who receive the order and remain in it permanently. In 1967, following the desire expressed by the bishops of Vatican II, Pope Paul VI decreed that (1) qualified unmarried men twenty-five years of age or older may be ordained permanent deacons, but may not marry after ordination; (2) qualified married men thirty-five years of age or older, with the consent of their wives, may be ordained permanent deacons. Of these deacons Vatican II declares: " . . . strengthened by sacramental grace, in communion with the bishop and his group of priests, they serve the People of God in the ministry of the liturgy, of the word, and of charity" (Dogmatic Constitution on the Church, #29).

DEAD SEA SCROLLS
A collection of manuscripts and fragments of manuscripts discovered in 1947 at the site of the ancient Qumran community west of the Dead Sea. They have been dated from approximately 100 years before and after Christ. Among the scrolls are portions of many Old Testament books and writings about the Essene community (an ascetical community or sect living in Palestine during the first century B.C. and the first century A.D.). The scrolls, which are still being studied, have been of great value to biblical scholars in reconstructing the textual history of the Old Testament.

DEATH
According to Christian teaching, death (that is, the cessation of life or the separation of the soul from the body) is considered a punishment for Adam's sin: "Therefore, just as through one man sin entered the world and with sin death, death thus coming to all men inasmuch as all sinned . . . '' (Romans 5:12). At the same time, however, Christian faith affirms that the power of death is not eternal but, because of the victorious Resurrection of Christ, yields to a new and eternal life: "If death began its reign through one man because of his offense, much more shall those who receive the overflowing grace and gift of justice live and reign through the one man, Jesus Christ" (Romans 5:17).

DECALOGUE
See COMMANDMENTS OF GOD.

DEPOSIT OF FAITH

A term used to describe the sum of revelation and tradition entrusted to the Church and its teaching office (magisterium) to be safeguarded and explained to the People of God. "The Roman Pontiff and the bishops, in conformity with their duty and as befits the gravity of the matter, strive painstakingly and by appropriate means to inquire properly into that revelation and to give apt expression to its contents. But they do not accept any new public revelation as part of the divine deposit of faith" (Dogmatic Constitution on the Church, #25).

DEVIL

An evil spirit or a fallen angel; specifically, the term often applies to Lucifer or Satan, the chief of the fallen angels (see Matthew 12:24), who tempts the human person to sin. In his teaching and ministry Jesus Christ opposes the evil spirit with the Spirit of God.

DIOCESE

According to the Code of Canon Law, "A diocese is a portion of the people of God which is entrusted for pastoral care to a bishop with the cooperation of the presbyterate so that, adhering to its pastor and gathered by him in the Holy Spirit through the gospel and the Eucharist, it constitutes a particular church in which the one, holy, catholic and apostolic Church of Christ is truly present and operative" (Canon 369). Only the Holy See is authorized to erect a diocese.

DISCIPLE

A word which means "learner," it is used to describe those who hear and follow the teaching of Jesus (Matthew 10:1), not only in New Testament times but in every age.

DIVINITY OF CHRIST

It is the solemn teaching of the Church that Jesus Christ is a divine Person, true God as well as true man, the second Person of the Blessed Trinity. See HOLY TRINITY.

DIVORCE

The teaching of the Church, based on the teaching of Christ himself (see Mark 10:2-12 and Luke 16:18) is that "A ratified and consummated marriage cannot be dissolved by any human power or for any reason other than death" (Canon 1141). Thus, although civil law may claim to dissolve the bond of marriage and render a person free to marry again, the Church maintains that the civil law has no power to do this. For serious reasons (such as adultery, serious danger to spirit or body of the other spouse or of the children), a spouse may have a legitimate cause for separation "in virtue of a decree of the local ordinary, or even on his or her own authority if there is danger in delay" (Canon 1153, §1). Concerning cases where a decree of nullity regarding a marriage may be granted by the Church, see ANNULMENT.

DOCTOR OF THE CHURCH
A title conferred on ecclesiastical writers of eminent learning and outstanding holiness because of their contribution to the explanation and defense of Catholic doctrine. There are presently 32 such Doctors of the Church, including two women, Saint Catherine of Siena (died 1380) and Saint Teresa of Avila (died 1582).

DOGMA
A teaching or doctrine authoritatively and explicitly proposed by the Church as revealed by God and requiring the belief of the People of God. A dogma may be proposed by the Church in a solemn manner (for example, the dogma of the Immaculate Conception) or through the ordinary magisterium (for example, the truth that innocent human life is inviolable).

DOXOLOGY
A hymn or prayer of glory and praise to God; notably, the "Glory to God in the highest" often prayed at Mass; the "Through him, with him, in him, etc." that concludes the Eucharistic Prayer; the "Glory be to the Father and to the Son and to the Holy Spirit. . . ."

DRUGS, MORALITY OF
Psychotropic (or psychoactive) drugs are chemicals that influence the working of the mind and alter behavior, mood, and mental functioning. These drugs may be distinguished into two main categories: therapeutic and nontherapeutic. The use of

therapeutic drugs is considered morally justified provided they are used under the direction of a competent physician and are believed to be for the total good of the patient. The use of nontherapeutic drugs is considered morally unjustified when they seriously impair one's health or human functioning or when there is danger of addiction.

E

EASTER

A movable feast, celebrated on a Sunday between March 22 and April 25, commemorating the Resurrection of Jesus Christ from the dead (see Mark 16:1-7). It is considered the greatest of all Christian feasts and holds a central place in the liturgical year. Liturgically, the celebration of Christ's Resurrection continues for a period of 50 days, that is, from Easter Sunday to the feast of Pentecost. See YEAR, LITURGICAL.

EASTER DUTY

A popular term for the obligation thus described in the Code of Canon Law. "All the faithful, after they have been initiated into the Most Holy Eucharist, are bound by the obligation of receiving Communion at least once a year.

"This precept must be fulfilled during the Easter season unless it is fulfilled for a just cause at some other time during the year" (Canon 920, §1 and §2).

In the United States the Easter season, for purposes of fulfilling this precept, has traditionally been understood to extend from the First Sunday of Lent until Trinity Sunday (eight weeks after Easter).

EASTER VIGIL

Called the "mother of all holy vigils," the Easter Vigil is celebrated after sundown on the night before Easter. The Easter Vigil service includes ceremonies that were held in the early Christian communities and highlights some of the most precious symbols of the Church. The Vigil consists of four parts: Service of the Light, Liturgy of the Word, Liturgy of Baptism, and Liturgy of the Eucharist.

EASTERN CHURCHES, CATHOLIC

These are Catholic Churches whose members (approximately 12 million throughout the world) follow the Eastern Rites. Originally, they were the Patriarchates of Constantinople, Alexandria, Antioch, and Jerusalem. Today the five principal rites are the Byzantine, Alexandrian, Antiochene, Armenian, and Chaldean. Best represented in the United States is the Byzantine Rite with nine dioceses serving its Ruthenian and Ukranian Rite adherents. Vatican Council II, in its Decree on Eastern Catholic Churches, says: "The Catholic Church holds in high esteem the institutions of the Eastern Churches, their liturgical rites, ecclesiastical traditions, and Christian way of life. For, distinguished as they are by their venerable antiquity, they are bright with that tradition which was handed down from the apostles through the Fathers, and which forms part of the divinely revealed and undivided heritage of the universal Church" (#1).

EASTERN CHURCHES, SEPARATED

These are the Eastern Churches that are not in union with Rome. Their separation occurred in 1054 in what is often historically referred to as the Eastern Schism. The Orthodox Churches are the largest of these separated Eastern Churches. They hold in common with their Eastern Catholic counterparts many matters of faith and morals, valid orders and sacraments, and a rich liturgy. They accept, however, only the first seven ecumenical councils of the Church, and they do not acknowledge or hold communion with the pope. Since Vatican Council II there has been a continuing ecumenical dialogue between the separated Eastern Churches and the Catholic Church.

ECCLESIASTES, BOOK OF

One of the Wisdom Books of the Old Testament, written by an unknown author around 250 B.C. Its essential theme is the vanity of all human efforts and achievements in relationship to lasting happiness; the wise person is the one who fears the Lord and keeps his commandments. See WISDOM BOOKS.

ECCLESIOLOGY

That part of theology which studies the nature, members, structure, and mission of the Church. See CHURCH.

ECUMENICAL COUNCIL

The word *ecumenical* means "general" or "universal"; an ecumenical council is an assembly of all Catholic bishops ("the college of bishops") together with and under the authority of the Bishop of Rome, the pope. According to the Code of Canon Law: "The college of bishops exercises power over the universal Church in a solemn manner in an ecumenical council" (Canon 337, §1). The authority of the pope in regard to ecumenical councils is stated thus by the Code of Canon Law: "It is for the Roman Pontiff alone to convoke an ecumenical council, to preside over it personally or through others, to transfer, suspend or dissolve it, and to approve its decrees" (Canon 338, §1). There have been 21 ecumenical councils in the history of the Church. See TRENT, COUNCIL OF; VATICAN COUNCIL I; VATICAN COUNCIL II.

ECUMENISM

The movement which seeks to bring about the unity of all Christians. According to Vatican Council II, "the 'ecumenical movement' means those activities and enterprises which, according to various needs of the Church and opportune occasions, are started and organized for the fostering of unity among Christians" (Decree on Ecumenism, #4).

EMMANUEL

A Hebrew word (sometimes spelled Immanuel) which literally translates as "God with us." It is found as a prophecy in Isaiah 7:14, and as part of the angelic message in Matthew 1:23:
The virgin shall be with child
and give birth to a son,
and they shall call him Emmanuel,
a name which means "God is with us."

ENCYCLICAL

A "circular letter" addressed by the pope to all members of the Church or to a specific group in the Church or, as is common for recent popes, to all men and women of good will. The subject matter of an encyclical is traditionally serious and important, a matter of doctrine or morals or discipline in the Church or a matter of grave importance (for example, peace, justice) to the whole world. For Catholics, the teachings in encyclicals "belong to the ordinary magisterium of the Church" (Pope Pius XII) and therefore demand internal assent and external respect. See MAGISTERIUM.

ENVY
One of the capital or "deadly" sins, it is sadness or melancholy at the gifts (natural or supernatural), good fortune, or success of another precisely because these are seen as a loss to oneself or a diminishment of one's own excellence; it is a violation of the virtue of charity.

EPIPHANY
A liturgical feast celebrated on January 6 (or in the United States on a Sunday between January 2 and January 8) commemorating the manifestation of Christ to the Gentiles in the person of the Magi and his divinity manifested at his Baptism as well as at the marriage feast of Cana. It is a feast of ancient origin, especially in the East, and in many countries is the occasion for special celebrations and the exchange of gifts.

EPISTLES
See LETTERS (NEW TESTAMENT).

ESCHATOLOGY
Eschata is Greek for "last things"; eschatology is that part of theology which studies "the last things," such as death, judgment, heaven, hell, purgatory, the resurrection of the body, the second coming of Christ.

EUCHARIST
One of the seven sacraments of the Church, indeed the greatest of the sacraments, described by the Church in this way: "The Most Holy Eucharist is the most august sacrament, in which Christ the Lord himself is contained, offered and received, and by which the Church constantly lives and grows. The Eucharistic Sacrifice, the memorial of the death and resurrection of the Lord, in which the sacrifice of the cross is perpetuated over the centuries, is the summit and the source of all Christian worship and life; it signifies and effects the unity of the people of God and achieves

the building up of the Body of Christ. The other sacraments and all the ecclesiastical works of the apostolate are closely related to the Holy Eucharist and are directed to it'' (Canon 897).

Although the Eucharist is one sacrament, there are three essential aspects to which the Church points: (1) It is a Sacrifice; in the words of Vatican Council II: ''At the Last Supper, on the night when He was betrayed, our Savior instituted the Eucharistic Sacrifice of His Body and Blood. He did this in order to perpetuate the sacrifice of the Cross throughout the centuries until He should come again . . . '' (Constitution on the Liturgy, #47). (2) It is a Communion; Christ himself, the Bread of Life, is really and truly present under the appearances of bread and wine and comes to the believer in Holy Communion as spiritual food. (3) It is Real Presence; for Christ himself is present in the Eucharistic species and abides among us, and is worthy of our adoration, gratitude, and love.

The Church calls the faithful to respond in faith to these three aspects of the Eucharist: ''The faithful are to hold the Eucharist in highest honor, taking part in the celebration of the Most August Sacrifice, receiving the sacrament devoutly and frequently, and worshiping it with supreme adoration . . . '' (Canon 898).

EUTHANASIA

From a Greek word which means ''easy death,'' euthanasia is now defined in a variety of ways. According to the Congregation for the Doctrine of the Faith in its *Declaration on Euthanasia* (1980), a strict definition is as follows: ''By euthanasia is understood an action or an omission which of itself and by intention causes death, in order that all suffering may in this way be eliminated.'' Concerning the morality of euthanasia defined in this way, the Declaration says: ''It is necessary to state firmly once more that nothing and no one can in any way permit the killing of an innocent human being, whether a fetus or an embryo, an infant or an adult, an older person or one suffering from an incurable disease, or a person who is dying. Furthermore, no one is permitted to ask for this act of killing, either for himself or herself or for another person entrusted to his or her care, nor can he or she consent to it, either explicitly or implicitly. Nor can any authority legitimately recommend or permit such an action. For it is a question of the divine law, an offense against the dignity of the human person, a crime against life, and an attack on humanity.''

EVANGELIZATION

The proclamation of the Gospel, especially to those people who have never heard it; concretely, according to Pope Paul VI in his magnificent letter on evangelization, "Evangelizing means to bring the Good News into all the strata of humanity, and through its influence transforming humanity from within and making it new. . . . But there is no new humanity if there are not first of all new persons renewed by baptism, and by lives lived according to the Gospel" (*Evangelization,* #18).

EVOLUTION

The scientific theory of organic evolution holds that existing forms of vegetable, animal, and human life developed from more primitive organisms; this theory has not been completely proven, and many questions remain. Even if it were to be proven beyond a shadow of a doubt, however, it does not necessarily stand in opposition to the Bible or Christian faith. While some Christian theologians and communities teach that evolutionary theory cannot be accepted by a Christian, others (including many Catholics) affirm that the theory may be judged on its own merits as long as there is no denial of the basic truth of revelation: namely, that God is the immediate Creator of the human soul. See SOUL.

EXCOMMUNICATION

A penalty imposed by the Church for serious offenses; by force of this penalty, as the Code of Canon Law points out, "An excommunicated person is forbidden: (1) to have any ministerial participation in celebrating the Eucharistic Sacrifice or in any other ceremonies whatsoever of public worship; (2) to celebrate the sacraments and sacramentals and to receive the sacraments; (3) to discharge any ecclesiastical offices, ministries or functions whatsoever, or to place acts of governance" (Canon 1331, §1).

EXODUS, BOOK OF

The second book of the Bible; the word *exodus* means "departure,'' and this book describes the departure of the Israelites from Egypt and their wandering through the desert to Mount Sinai. Five parts are discernible in this book: events in Egypt before the Exodus, leaving Egypt and journeying to Mount Sinai, the promulgation of the Mosaic law, reconciliation and renewal of the covenant, construction of the Tabernacle.

F

FAITH

One of the three theological (God-given and God-directed) virtues or powers, infused into the soul with sanctifying grace, by which, in the words of Vatican Council I, "a person is enabled to believe that what God has revealed is true — not because its intrinsic worth is seen with the rational light of reason — but because of the authority of God who reveals it, that God who can neither deceive nor be deceived." This definition is amplified by the description of faith given by Vatican Council II: " 'The obedience of faith' (see Romans 1:5; Romans 16:26; 2 Corinthians 10:5-6) must be given to God who reveals, an obedience by which man entrusts his whole self freely to God, offering 'the full submission of intellect and will to God who reveals,' and freely assenting to the truth revealed by Him. If this faith is to be shown, the grace of God and the interior help of the Holy Spirit must precede and assist, moving the heart and turning it to God, opening the eyes of the mind, and giving 'joy and ease to everyone in assenting to the truth and believing it.' To bring about an ever deeper understanding of revelation, the same Holy Spirit constantly brings faith to completion by His gifts" (Divine Revelation, #5).

FALL

A term used to describe the original sin of Adam and Eve as described in Genesis. See ORIGINAL SIN.

FAMILY, CHRISTIAN

Considering the family from a Christian viewpoint, Pope John Paul II, in his encyclical *Familiaris Consortio (On the Family)*, points out that the family is: (1) a community of persons: a community which must strive for ever deeper communion through the power of love; (2) a school of humanity where each member learns to take care of the others and where mutual service is highlighted; (3) a place of reconciliation where conflict and division can be healed; (4) a vital cell of society where young citizens learn the values of justice, respect, and charity.

FAMILY PLANNING, NATURAL
See NATURAL FAMILY PLANNING.

FAMILY, RIGHTS OF
The family is a natural society in its own right. As such it possesses certain fundamental rights which should be respected both by other natural societies and by individuals. After the Roman Synod of 1981, at which bishops from different parts of the world shared their views on the family, Pope John Paul II issued "a charter of family rights." These rights are as follows:

• The right to exist and progress as a family, that is, the right of every human being, even if he or she is poor, to found a family and to have adequate means to support it.
• The right to exercise its responsibility regarding the transmission of life and to educate children.
• The right to the intimacy of conjugal life.
• The right to the stability of the bond and the institution of marriage.
• The right to believe in and profess one's faith and to propagate it.
• The right to bring up children in accord with the family's own traditions and religious values, with the necessary instruments, means, and institutions.
• The right, especially of the poor and sick, to obtain physical, social, political, and economic security.
• The right to housing suitable for living family life in a suitable way.
• The right to expression and representation, either directly or through associations, before the economic, social, and cultural public authorities.
• The right to form associations with other families and institutions in order to fulfill the family's role suitably.
• The right to protect minors by adequate legislation from harmful drugs, pornography, and the like.

- The right to wholesome recreation of a kind that also fosters family values.
- The right of the elderly to a worthy life and a worthy death.
- The right to emigrate as a family in search of a better life.

FASTING

A traditional form of penance among religious people, seen as a way of purifying the spirit or of sacrificing some good to the Lord; it consists in one's free choice to limit the kind or quantity of food or drink. The Gospel emphasizes, especially, the motivation for fasting: namely, that it be done not for vain display but as expression of interior religious attitudes (see Matthew 6:1-18). According to the general law of the Church, Catholics (from the completion of their eighteenth year to the completion of their fifty-ninth) are obliged to fast on Ash Wednesday and on Good Friday. The law of fasting allows only one full meal a day, but does not prohibit taking some food in the morning and evening. See ABSTINENCE.

FATHERS OF THE CHURCH

Saintly, orthodox writers of the early Church (from the first to approximately the end of the seventh century); their writings had a major impact on the doctrinal development of the Church. They are usually divided into the Latin Fathers, including such giants as Saint Irenaeus (130-200), Saint Ambrose (340-397), Saint Augustine (354-430), and the Greek Fathers, including Saint Clement of Alexandria (150-215), Saint Athanasius (297-373), Saint John Chrysostom (347-407).

FATIMA

See SHRINES OF OUR LADY.

FORNICATION

Sexual intercourse between a man and a woman who are not married. According to Christian tradition, clearly stated in the New Testament (see, for example, Ephesians 5:1-7 and 1 Thessalonians 4:3-8), fornication is morally wrong. This tradition was aptly summarized by the American Catholic bishops in their pastoral reflections on the moral life, *To Live in Christ Jesus*: "Our Christian tradition holds the sexual union between husband

and wife in high honor, regarding it as a special expression of their covenanted love which mirrors God's love for His people and Christ's love for the Church. But like many things human, sex is ambivalent. It can be either creative or destructive. Sexual intercourse is a moral and human good only within marriage; outside marriage it is wrong.'' See CHASTITY.

FORTITUDE
One of the four cardinal (or "hinge") virtues and one of the gifts of the Holy Spirit; it is courage in doing good despite the dangers or difficulties that stand in one's way.

FREEDOM, HUMAN
According to the teaching of the Church, the human person, made in the image and likeness of God, is not subject to determinism but possesses true moral freedom of choice: that is, the human person, when acting in a truly human way, is able to choose or not to choose a certain course of action or is able to choose freely between two alternative courses of action. The importance of human freedom is emphasized in Vatican Council II: "Only in freedom can man direct himself toward goodness. . . . authentic freedom is an exceptional sign of the divine image within man . . . Hence man's dignity demands that he act according to a knowing and free choice. Such a choice is personally motivated and prompted from within. It does not result from blind internal impulse nor from mere external pressure'' (Pastoral Constitution on the Church in the Modern World, #17).

FREEDOM OF CONSCIENCE
The dignity of the human person consists in the fact that he or she can intelligently and freely choose God's will and God's law. On a practical level, conscience plays a critical role in this choice. Conscience should be free from all external constraints and force. According to Vatican Council II: " . . . man perceives and acknowledges the imperatives of the divine law through the mediation of conscience. In all his activity a man is bound to follow his conscience faithfully, in order that he may come to God, for whom he was created. It follows that he is not to be forced to act in a manner contrary to his conscience. Nor, on the

other hand, is he to be restrained from acting in accordance with his conscience, especially in matters religious'' (Declaration on Religious Freedom, #3).

FREEDOM, RELIGIOUS
In matters of religious conviction and worship of God the human person should be free to follow the dictates of his or her own conscience and should not be forced by civil authority to act against these dictates nor be restrained from acting in accord with them, provided there is no serious danger to the common good. Vatican Council II in its Declaration on Religious Freedom points out that the right to religious freedom in civil society "means that all men are to be immune from coercion on the part of individuals or of social groups and of any human power, in such wise that in matters religious no one is to be forced to act in a manner contrary to his own beliefs. Nor is anyone to be restrained from acting in accordance with his own beliefs, whether privately or publicly, whether alone or in association with others, within due limits . . ." (Religious Freedom, #2).

FUNDAMENTALISTS
This term is used to refer to a variety of Protestant individuals or communities; generally speaking, fundamentalists are conservative evangelicals who insist on the literal interpretation of the Scriptures, place great emphasis on the "born again" experience, the second coming of Christ, and personal missionary activity. They tend to be quite critical of liberal Protestant churches and of the Catholic Church.

FUNERAL RITES
The liturgical ceremonies that the Church provides for her deceased members, including the Mass of Christian Burial, the final commendation, and prayers at the grave; the emphasis is on Christian hope, resurrection, and eternal life. See BURIAL, ECCLESIASTICAL; CREMATION; WAKE.

G

GALATIANS
See LETTERS (NEW TESTAMENT).

GAMBLING
In Catholic moral theology, gambling is considered a kind of contract (technically, an aleatory contract, from the Latin word *alea* meaning "chance"). It is a contract by which the participants in a game of chance agree that the winner receives a certain prize or sum of money. Though some Christian churches condemn gambling absolutely, the Catholic tradition has held that it may be morally justified provided the following conditions are observed: (*a*) the stakes belong to the one who gambles and may be freely used by him or her; (*b*) there is no fraud or deceit involved, such as marked cards, loaded dice, collusion with the operator; (*c*) there is equal risk and equal opportunity for all participants; (*d*) there is no just prohibition by the civil authorities. At the same time, Catholic moralists warn that gambling can give rise to serious abuses, especially for those who are compulsive or addictive gamblers; without regulation by civil law, it is often taken over by gangster elements.

GENESIS, BOOK OF
The first book of the Bible; the first eleven chapters treat of the origin of the world and the human race, the original state of innocence and the Fall, the promise of salvation, the Deluge, the Tower of Babel; the remaining chapters treat the early history of Israel, especially outstanding leaders, such as Abraham, Isaac, Jacob, and Joseph.

GENTILES
A word used frequently in the Bible, it means "pagans" or "foreigners" or simply people who were not Jews. In the Old Testament there is evidence of hostility and distrust between Jews

and Gentiles. In the New Testament it is clear that Jesus first directed his disciples to preach the Good News only to "the lost sheep of the house of Israel" (Matthew 10:5), but gradually extended their mission to the Gentiles — "all nations" — as well (see Matthew 28:19). The extension of the Church to Gentiles is spoken of in Acts of the Apostles (see chapters 8 to 12) and in many of the New Testament Letters.

GENUFLECTION
A bending of the knee as a sign of adoration or reverence; it is a Catholic practice to genuflect when entering a Church where the Blessed Sacrament is reserved or when passing before the Blessed Sacrament.

GIFTS OF THE HOLY SPIRIT
According to Catholic teaching, the gifts of the Holy Spirit are supernatural graces freely given to the soul with sanctifying grace and enable the graced person to respond freely and promptly to the inspirations of God. The seven gifts of the Holy Spirit are wisdom, understanding, counsel, fortitude, knowledge, piety, and fear of the Lord.

GLUTTONY
One of the capital or "deadly" sins, it is an unreasonable, disordered desire for food and drink, usually expressed by eating or drinking to excess. See TEMPERANCE.

GOD
Catholic teaching on the nature of God and his divine attributes is admirably expressed by Vatican Council I: "The holy, Catholic, apostolic Roman Church believes and professes that there is one true, living God, the Creator and Lord of heaven and earth. He is almighty, eternal, beyond measure, incomprehensible, and infinite in intellect, will and every perfection. Since he is one unique spiritual substance, entirely simple and unchangeable, he must be declared distinct from the world, perfectly happy in himself and by his very nature, and inexpressibly exalted over all things that exist or can be conceived other than himself." In the fullness of revelation, moreover, it is known that the one God subsists in three equal persons, the Father and the Son and the Holy Spirit. See HOLY TRINITY.

GODPARENT

See BAPTISMAL SPONSOR.

GOSPEL

From an Old English word *god-spel,* that is, good news, a Gospel is one of the four divinely inspired accounts of the life, teaching, suffering, death, and Resurrection of Jesus Christ. It is customary to describe the Gospels of Matthew, Mark, and Luke as "Synoptic Gospels" because they give a "synopsis" or similar view of the life and teaching of Jesus; the Gospel of John reflects a different apostolic tradition. The Gospels are held in high esteem by the Church; passages from them are read in the Eucharistic liturgy and in the formal celebration of all the sacraments. See MATTHEW; MARK; LUKE; JOHN.

GRACE

A biblical and theological term used in a wide variety of ways. According to Catholic teaching, grace is a supernatural gift of God bestowed upon a person with a view to salvation and sanctification. Understood in this sense, there are three kinds of grace: (1) uncreated grace refers to the abiding presence of the Holy Trinity in the souls of the just; (2) created or sanctifying grace is a created sharing or participation in the life of God himself; (3) actual grace is a transient help of God which enlightens the mind and strengthens the will to do good and avoid evil. Grace is given to human beings through the merits of Jesus Christ and is communicated by the Holy Spirit. The principal means of growing in grace are prayer, the sacraments (especially the Eucharist), and good works. Sanctifying grace is lost by the commission of mortal sin.

GUADALUPE, OUR LADY OF

See SHRINES OF OUR LADY.

GUILT

A state or condition of mind and soul that follows upon a personal, free, deliberate transgression of God's law; awareness that one has done wrong gives rise to what are often referred to as "guilt feelings," that is, feelings of spiritual unrest and discomfort that seek relief. Guilt feelings, in their turn, urge the sinful person to repent and to seek reconciliation, and thus once again to experience inner peace. In contrast to true guilt which follows upon actual sin, false or neurotic guilt seems to arise from a general lack of self-worth or a scrupulous conviction that one is almost always in sin.

H

HAIL MARY

The best-known and most popular prayer in honor of the Blessed Virgin Mary, it is composed of verses from the Gospel of Luke (see Luke 1:28,42) and a centuries-old petition formulated by the Church. "Hail Mary, full of grace. The Lord is with thee. Blessed art thou amongst women, and blessed is the fruit of thy womb, Jesus. Holy Mary, Mother of God, pray for us sinners, now and at the hour of our death. Amen."

HEAVEN

The dwelling place of God and the angels and the place of eternal happiness for all those who have been saved; it consists primarily in the beatific vision, the face-to-face vision of God, the possession of eternal life and peace; in addition, the blessed in heaven rejoice in the knowledge, love, and enjoyment of creatures.

HEBREWS, LETTER TO THE

See LETTERS (NEW TESTAMENT).

HELL

The dwelling place of Satan and the evil spirits and of all those who die deliberately alienated from God. The primary punishment of hell is the pain of loss: the deprivation of the face-to-face vision of God and eternal happiness with him. There is also the pain of sense caused by an outside agent, described as fire in the New Testament (see Matthew 25:41 and Mark 9:43). Hell is the dire destination for one who freely chooses his or her own will against the will of God.

HERESY

Formal heresy is the deliberate and obstinate denial by a baptized person of any truth which must be believed as a matter of divine and Catholic faith; it is a grave sin and incurs the penalty of excommunication (see Canon 1364, §1). Reference is sometimes made to "material heresy" as the condition of those baptized persons who, in good faith and through no fault of their own, accept heretical doctrine; but, since they are in good faith, in reality there is no sin and no excommunication. See EX-COMMUNICATION.

HIERARCHY

This term, as applied to the systematic arrangement of authority within the Catholic Church, is used in two ways: (1) the hierarchy of Holy Orders: namely, those ordained as bishops, priests, or deacons to carry out the sacramental and pastoral ministry of the Church; and (2) the hierarchy of jurisdiction: namely, the pope and the bishops in communion with him to carry out, by divine institution, the teaching and governing office in the Church. Vatican Council II treats of this entire matter in chapter 3 of the Dogmatic Constitution on the Church.

HOLY DAYS OF OBLIGATION

Days especially set aside for the worship of God: notably, each Sunday of the year and other feast days designated by the Church. According to the Code of Canon Law: "Sunday is the day on which the paschal mystery is celebrated in light of the apostolic tradition and is to be observed as the foremost holy day of obligation in the universal Church. Also to be observed are the day of the Nativity of Our Lord Jesus Christ, the Epiphany, the Ascension and the Most Holy Body and Blood of Christ, Holy Mary Mother of God and her Immaculate Conception and Assumption, Saint Joseph, the Apostles Saints Peter and Paul, and finally, All Saints" (Canon 1246, §1). The Code then goes on to note this practical principle: "However, the conference of bishops can abolish certain holy days of obligation or transfer them to a Sunday with prior approval of the Apostolic See" (Canon 1246, §2). The holy days to be observed in the United States are the Nativity of Our Lord Jesus Christ (December 25), Solemnity of Mary the Mother of God (January 1), Ascension of the Lord (sixth Thursday after Easter), Assumption of the Virgin Mary (August 15), All Saints (November 1), Immaculate Conception of the Virgin Mary (December 8). (In Canada, Christmas and New Year's Day are holy days. Others formerly specified have either been made nonobligatory or transferred to the Sunday following.)

The obligation of Catholics on these holy days is as follows: "On Sundays and other holy days of obligation the faithful are bound to participate in the Mass; they are also to abstain from those labors and business concerns which impede the worship to be rendered to God, the joy which is proper to the Lord's Day, or the proper relaxation of mind and body" (Canon 1247).

HOLY ORDERS, SACRAMENT OF

One of the seven sacraments of the Church, it is defined thus in the Code of Canon Law: "By divine institution some among the Christian faithful are constituted sacred ministers through the sacrament of orders by means of the indelible character with which they are marked; accordingly they are consecrated and deputed to shepherd the people of God, each in accord with his own grade of orders, by fulfilling in the person of Christ the Head the functions of teaching, sanctifying and governing" (Canon 1008). "The orders are the episcopacy, the presbyterate [priesthood], and the diaconate" (Canon 1009, §1) See BISHOP; PRIEST; DEACON.

HOLY SPIRIT

The third Person of the Holy Trinity, distinct from the Father and the Son but coequal and coeternal with them. The ancient faith of the Church concerning the Holy Spirit — professed in all of the Christian creeds — is beautifully summarized in Pope Paul VI's Credo of the People of God: "We believe in the Holy Spirit, who is Lord and giver of life, who is adored and glorified with the Father and the Son. He spoke to us by the prophets; he was sent by Christ after his resurrection and his ascension to the Father; he illuminates, vivifies, protects and guides the Church."

HOLY TRINITY

The most sublime and central doctrine of the Christian faith, namely, that there are three Persons — Father, Son, Holy Spirit — in one God. This doctrine is indicated in the Scriptures (see, for example, Matthew 28:18-20) and expressed in all of the

Christian creeds. The Catholic Church celebrates the feast of the
Holy Trinity on the Sunday after Pentecost.

HOLY WATER
Water that is blessed by a priest for use by the People of God,
ordinarily while one is blessing oneself with the sign of the cross;
it is a symbol of spiritual cleansing and by custom is used in time
of physical or spiritual dangers; it is used in all of the Church's
blessings. See BLESSING; SACRAMENTALS.

HOLY WEEK
The week before Easter, it is called "the great week" of the
Church's liturgical year; it begins with Passion (Palm) Sunday,
celebrating Christ's entrance into Jerusalem to accomplish his
Paschal mystery (see John 12:12), and also includes the Easter
Triduum: Holy Thursday, commemorating the institution of the
Holy Eucharist and the institution of the priesthood; Good Fri-
day, commemorating the Passion and death of Jesus Christ; and
the Easter Vigil, celebrating his Resurrection. See EASTER VIGIL.

HOMILY
An integral part of the Mass, it is an instruction or sermon
preached after the readings from Scripture; its purpose is to
explain the word of God and also to make application of that word
to the lives of people today.

HOMOSEXUALITY, MORALITY OF
Sexual attraction to or relationship with members of one's own
sex; concerning the moral dimensions of homosexuality, Catholic
teaching distinguishes between homosexual orientation and
homosexual activity, a distinction expressed in the American
bishops' letter on the moral life: "Some persons find themselves
through no fault of their own to have a homosexual orientation.
Homosexuals, like everyone else, should not suffer from preju-
dice against their basic human rights. They have a right to
respect, friendship, and justice. They should have an active role
in the Christian community. Homosexual activity, however, as
distinguished from homosexual orientation, is morally wrong.
Like heterosexual persons, homosexuals are called to give witness to chastity, avoiding, with God's grace, behavior which is

wrong for them, just as nonmarital sexual relations are wrong for heterosexuals'' (*To Live in Christ Jesus*).

HOPE
One of the theological (God-given and God-directed) virtues or powers, infused into the soul with sanctifying grace, by which we are able confidently to expect eternal life, the fullness of glory with God, and all the means to attain it, because God is faithful to his promises.

HUMILITY
The moral virtue by which one recognizes his or her absolute dependence on God, appreciates all of one's abilities and talents as gifts of God, and strives to use them in accord with his will and purpose.

I

ICON

The Greek word for "image"; an icon is an image of our Lord, our Lady, or one of the saints, painted or glazed on a flat surface and used in Eastern churches in place of statues.

ICONOCLASM

A heresy that arose in the eighth century declaring that the religious veneration of pictures or images was sacriligious and advocating "image breaking" as a solution to the problem; in 787, at the Second Council of Nicea, the Church, while defining the distinction between adoration to be given to God alone and veneration paid to Mary or the other saints, declared that such veneration is, in reality, an act of piety not toward the image but toward the person represented.

IDOLATRY

Giving to any creature the worship that is due to the one true God alone; it is a violation of the first commandment.

IGNATIUS LOYOLA, SAINT

Born in 1491, he was a Spanish soldier wounded in the battle of Pamplona in 1521; during his recuperation he received an extraordinary grace of conversion, gave up his military career, and committed himself in a special way to Christ and the Church; he founded the Society of Jesus (Jesuits) in 1534 and composed the world-famous *Spiritual Exercises;* he died in 1556 and was canonized in 1622; his feast day is celebrated on July 31.

IMMACULATE CONCEPTION

A belief of ancient origin in the Church, defined as a dogma in 1854 by Pope Pius IX in these words: "We declare, announce, and define that the doctrine which states that the Blessed Virgin Mary was preserved, in the first instant of her conception, by a singular grace and privilege of God omnipotent and because of the merits of Jesus Christ the Savior of the human race, free from all stain of original sin, is revealed by God and must be believed firmly and with constancy by all the faithful." The feast of Mary's Immaculate Conception is celebrated on December 8 and is a holy day of obligation for the universal Church.

IMPEDIMENTS TO MARRIAGE
An impediment is an obstacle; according to the Code of Canon Law there are certain obstacles to a valid marriage. These are called "diriment impediments." The Code defines a diriment impediment in this way: "A diriment impediment renders a person incapable of contracting marriage validly" (Canon 1073). The Code lists these impediments in Canons 1083 to 1094. Ordinarily, a person may receive a dispensation from impediments arising from ecclesiastical (Church) law, provided there is sufficient reason, by requesting it from one's diocesan bishop; in several cases, however, only the Holy See can grant a dispensation. Impediments arising from natural law (for example, impotence) cannot be given a dispensation.

IMPOTENCE
The inability to perform the sexual act of intercourse; it is called antecedent impotence when it existed before the marriage; it is called perpetual when it cannot be corrected without serious danger to health or life. According to the Code of Canon Law, "Antecedent and perpetual impotence to have intercourse, whether on the part of the man or of the woman, which is either absolute or relative, of its very nature invalidates marriage" (Canon 1084, §1). See STERILITY.

INCARNATION OF JESUS CHRIST
The basic Christian doctrine which affirms that Jesus Christ, the eternal Son of God, the second Person of the Holy Trinity, took human flesh from his human mother Mary and that he is at one and the same time fully God and fully man. There are two natures, human and divine, permanently united in the one divine Person, Jesus Christ.

INCENSE

A grainy substance made from the resins of various plants that gives off an aromatic odor when burned; used in divine worship as a symbol of the ascent of prayer to God.

INDULGENCE

According to the Code of Canon Law, "An indulgence is a remission before God of the temporal punishment for sin the guilt of which is already forgiven, which a properly disposed member of the Christian faithful obtains under certain and definite conditions with the help of the Church which, as the minister of redemption, dispenses and applies authoritatively the treasury of the satisfactions of Christ and the saints" (Canon 992). The Code also notes that "An indulgence is either partial or plenary in as far as it frees from the temporal punishment due to sin either partly or totally" (Canon 993) and that "The faithful can gain partial or plenary indulgences for themselves or apply them for the dead by way of suffrage" (Canon 994). The most complete modern teaching of the Church on indulgences is found in the Apostolic Constitution on Indulgences issued by Pope Paul VI after Vatican Council II (1967). See PURGATORY; TEMPORAL PUNISHMENT.

INERRANCY OF SCRIPTURE

The teaching of the Church concerning the truth of the the Sacred Scriptures, expressed by Vatican Council II in this way: "Therefore, since everything asserted by the inspired authors or sacred writers must be held to be asserted by the Holy Spirit, it follows that the books of Scripture must be acknowledged as teaching firmly, faithfully, and without error that truth which God wanted put into the sacred writings for the sake of our salvation" (Dogmatic Constitution on Divine Revelation, #11). See INSPIRATION, BIBLICAL.

INFALLIBILITY

A doctrine of the Church that the Church, through the power of God, is preserved from the possibility and liability of error in teaching matters of faith and morals. This charism is present in a singular way in the Bishop of Rome — the pope — and in the college of bishops. This doctrine is carefully described by Vatican Council II in its Dogmatic Constitution on the Church: "This infallibility with which the divine Redeemer willed His Church to be endowed in defining a doctrine of faith and morals extends as far as extends the deposit of divine revelation, which must be religiously guarded and faithfully expounded. This is the infallibility which the Roman Pontiff, the head of the college of bishops, enjoys in virtue of his office, when, as the supreme shepherd and teacher of all the faithful, who confirms his brethren in their faith (see Luke 22:32), he proclaims by a definitive act some doctrine of faith or morals. Therefore his definitions, of themselves, and not from the consent of the Church, are justly styled irreformable, for they are pronounced with the assistance of the Holy Spirit, an assistance promised to him in blessed Peter. Therefore they need no approval of others, nor do they allow an appeal to any other judgment. For then the Roman Pontiff is not pronouncing judgment as a private person. Rather, as the supreme teacher of the universal Church, as one in whom the charism of the infallibility of the Church herself is individually present, he is expounding or defending a doctrine of Catholic faith.

"The infallibility promised to the Church resides also in the body of bishops when that body exercises supreme teaching authority with the successor of Peter. To the resultant definitions the assent of the Church can never be wanting, on account of the activity of that same Holy Spirit, whereby the whole flock of Christ is preserved and progresses in unity of faith" (#25).

INFANT BAPTISM
See BAPTISM OF INFANTS.

INQUISITION
Historically, a legal court of the Church whose purpose was to investigate and prosecute persons guilty of formal heresy. The Inquisition properly so-called came into existence in 1232; its main purpose was to call those professing heresy to repentance. There were a number of safeguards for the accused, including the right to counsel. If the heretic repented, an ordinary penance such as fasting was imposed. If the heretic did not repent, he then received a more severe penance such as the confiscation of goods or imprisonment or even death at the stake. Unfortunately — and

this was especially true in the Spanish Inquisition toward the end of the fifteenth century — the rights of the accused were not always respected; and penalties, including death, seemed to be imposed too rashly. Some modern historians believe that the abuses of the Inquisition — though sometimes exaggerated by enemies of the Church — crept into the process because the Church was too closely affiliated with the State. See HERESY.

INSPIRATION, BIBLICAL

The teaching of the Church, as expressed in Vatican II, that "Those divinely revealed realities which are contained and presented in sacred Scripture have been committed to writing under the inspiration of the Holy Spirit. Holy Mother Church, relying on the belief of the apostles, holds that the books of both the Old and New Testament in their entirety, with all their parts, are sacred and canonical because, having been written under the inspiration of the Holy Spirit (see John 20:31; 2 Timothy 3:16; 2 Peter 1:19-21; 3:15-16) they have God as their author and have been handed on as such to the Church herself. In composing the sacred books, God chose men and while employed by Him they made use of their powers and abilities, so that with Him acting in them and through them, they, as true authors, consigned to writing everything and only those things which He wanted" (Divine Revelation, #11).

ISAIAH, BOOK OF

Perhaps the best-known and greatest of the Prophetic Books of the Old Testament; Isaiah of Jerusalem was born about 760 B.C., and his career spanned the reign of three Judean kings; this book is beautifully written, contains many poems and oracles and outstanding prophecies, especially those concerning Immanuel (chapters 6-12). Chapters 40 to 55 are often referred to as Second Isaiah because they were written at a later date not by Isaiah of Jerusalem but by one of his followers; this section contains the four famous Servant Songs which the Church sees as applying to Jesus the Messiah.

J

JANSENISM

A body of heretical doctrine developed by Cornelius Jansen (1585-1638), a Catholic theologian and bishop, and his followers; in his book, *The Augustinus,* Jansen taught that when God first created human beings he made them good, but after the Fall human nature became a slave of sin and could no longer do any good on its own; the necessary grace to do good, however, was given only to the elect few (the predestined) for whom Jesus died; the sign that one belonged to the elect was a spirit of fear that kept the person from approaching the sacraments or feeling at peace with God. The followers of Jansen became extreme rigorists, taught that the average Catholic cannot keep some of the commandments and is practically always unworthy of receiving Holy Communion. This harsh and inhuman heresy was condemned by Pope Innocent X in 1653, but it exercised a strong negative influence on the pastoral life of the Church for centuries to come.

JEREMIAH, BOOK OF

One of the Prophetic Books of the Old Testament, written by Jeremiah who was born about 650 B.C. and called to his task at a young age; Jeremiah's writings express a keen awareness of the general idolatry and infidelity on the part of the Israelites and the external threats from their enemies; about the time Jerusalem was being destroyed (587 B.C.), Jeremiah uttered the great oracle of the "new" covenant (31:31-34), Yahweh's tender and consoling promise to his people; after the fall of Jerusalem, Jeremiah was forced into Egyptian exile and was probably murdered by his own countrymen.

JERUSALEM

An ancient city in Palestine that became the religious and political center of Israel, chosen by King David as his capital; three great temples were built in Jerusalem before the coming of Christ who, together with his apostles, ministered in Jerusalem; the city and the temple were destroyed in A.D. 70. The Church is sometimes referred to in the liturgy as the New Jerusalem.

JESUS

The name of our Lord, derived from a Hebrew name meaning "Yahweh is salvation"; given by divine command to Jesus "because he will save his people from their sins" (Matthew 1:21). See CHRIST.

JOB, BOOK OF

One of the Wisdom Books of the Old Testament, written by an unknown author between 600 and 400 B.C. Job is the chief character in several dialogues with his friends on the profound question of human suffering and how this evil can be reconciled with the goodness of God; the religious truth of this book is that, while there is no adequate human explanation of the mystery of evil or suffering, faith in God and submission to his will make them bearable.

JOHN, GOSPEL OF

One of the four divinely inspired accounts of the life, teaching, death, and Resurrection of Jesus Christ; written about A.D. 95, its author was traditionally considered to be John, the beloved apostle, but in the light of modern research is commonly considered to be one of John's disciples; it is the most theological of the Gospels, emphasizes the messiahship and divinity of Jesus, and roots the belief and practice of Christians in the person of Jesus who is the Word, the Way, the Truth, the Life, the Light.

JOSEPH, SAINT

Spouse of the Virgin Mary and foster father of Jesus; most of what we know about him is from the Gospel accounts, especially of Matthew and Luke, where he is described as a just or holy man; he has long been held in veneration by the Church, is honored as her universal patron on the feast of Saint Joseph, March 19, and as the special patron of working people on the feast of Saint Joseph the Worker, May 1.

JUDAISM

The oldest known religion of the Western World, it was revealed by God and originated with the Mosaic covenant (see Exodus 19:5-6) and was identified with the land of Israel (see Deuteronomy 11:8-9); Judaism does not have a formal creed, but traditionally expresses belief in one God who reveals himself through the law, the prophets, and the events of history; the faithful Jew is one who lives justly according to the law and who worships God by prayer, reflection upon the sacred writings, and the observance of Sabbath and other festivals. According to Vatican Council II, there is a relationship between the Church and the Jewish people, "the people to whom the covenants and the promises were given and from whom Christ was born according to the flesh (see Romans 9:4-5). On account of their fathers, this people remains most dear to God, for God does not repent of the gifts He makes . . ." (Dogmatic Constitution on the Church, #16).

JUDGMENT

According to Catholic teaching, there is a distinction between the General Judgment and particular judgment. The General or Last or Final Judgment is the judgment of the human race by Jesus Christ (see Matthew 25:31; 2 Thessalonians 2:3-10) who "will come again in glory to judge the living and the dead" (Nicene Creed). The particular judgment is the judgment that takes place immediately after an individual's death and determines whether the individual is worthy of heaven (after purification in purgatory, if necessary) or hell.

JUSTICE

One of the principal (cardinal) moral virtues; in the strictest sense, it is the virtue by which one person renders to another that which is his or her due, or the virtue which urges one to give to others what is theirs by right. Justice is required not only between person and person but also between individual persons and the community and likewise between the leaders of the community and the community itself. See SOCIAL JUSTICE.

JUSTIFICATION

The process by which a sinner is made right with God; in the teachings of Saint Paul, God makes a person "just," free from sin, and pleasing to God through grace, attested by faith (see Romans 3:20-30); according to formal Catholic teaching as expressed by the Council of Trent: "Justification is the change from the condition in which a person is born as a child of the first Adam into a state of grace and adoption among the children of God through the second Adam, Jesus Christ our Savior." Thus, justification includes a true removal of sin by the power of God and a true supernatural sanctification through the gift of sanctifying grace or participation in the life of God.

JUST WAGE
See WAGE, JUST.

JUST WAR
See WAR, MORALITY OF.

K

KERYGMA

From the Greek word for "proclamation"; in the Christian sense, it refers especially to the preaching of the Good News of salvation, the proclaiming of the essential elements of God's salvific plan in Christ, the passing on of the "core message" of the Gospel.

KEYS, POWER OF

The symbol of spiritual power and authority conferred on Saint Peter and his successors by Jesus Christ: "I will give to you the keys of the kingdom of heaven" (Matthew 16:19). The "power of the keys" is an expression used to describe the authority of the Bishop of Rome, the pope, over all the faithful and all the churches. It is also used to describe the Church's authority to "bind" or "loose" (forgive or retain) sins in the sacrament of Penance. See POPE; PRIMACY, PAPAL.

KINGDOM OF GOD

A rich biblical term, often translated as "the reign of God"; the coming of the kingdom of God was foretold in the Old Testament and was especially revealed in the very person of Christ, Son of God and Son of Man (see Mark 1:15; Matthew 4:17); in the words, works, and miracles of Christ, the kingdom is described (see, for example, Luke 11:20 and Matthew 12:28). The mission of the Church, in the words of Vatican II, is "to proclaim and to establish among all peoples the kingdom of Christ and of God. She becomes on earth the initial budding forth of that kingdom. While she slowly grows, the Church strains toward the consummation of the kingdom and, with all her strength, hopes and desires to be united in glory with her King" (Dogmatic Constitution on the Church, #5). The Church celebrates the feast of Christ the King on the final Sunday of the liturgical year.

KINGS, BOOKS OF

The First Book of Kings and the Second Book of Kings are Historical Books of the Old Testament, probably completed in the sixth century B.C. and covering a broad sweep of the history of Israel; included in these books are a description of the last days of David, the reign of Solomon, the building of the Temple, stories concerning the prophets Elijah and Elisha, the destruction of Jerusalem and the Temple. One of the theological themes running through these books is that the tragedies which occurred among the people were due to their weak faith and their lack of fidelity to God's law.

L

LABOR

See WORK.

LAITY

All members of the Church belong to the People of God, the Christian faithful. According to the Code of Canon Law: "The Christian faithful are those who, inasmuch as they have been incorporated in Christ through baptism, have been constituted as the people of God; for this reason, since they have become sharers in Christ's priestly, prophetic and royal office in their own manner, they are called to exercise the mission which God has entrusted to the Church to fulfill in the world, in accord with the condition proper to each one" (Canon 204, §1). Among the Christian faithful the laity are all the faithful except those in Holy Orders (clergy) and those who belong to a religious state approved by the Church (religious). According to Vatican Council II's Decree on the Apostolate of the Laity (#8), the special mission of the laity is to renew the temporal order and to witness to Christ in a special way amid secular affairs.

LA SALETTE

See SHRINES OF OUR LADY.

LAST SUPPER

The traditional name given to the Passover meal which Jesus ate with his apostles in Jerusalem on the night before he died (see Mark 14:15; Luke 22:12). According to Catholic teaching, it was on this occasion that Jesus instituted the Holy Eucharist and the holy priesthood. The Church celebrates the Mass of the Lord's Supper on Holy Thursday evening.

LAST THINGS

See ESCHATOLOGY.

LAW

As used in Catholic theology, the term "law" is used in several senses, the most important of which are as follows:

The Eternal Law: that is, the plan of divine wisdom insofar as it directs all activity and all change toward a final end; the eternal and universal law whereby, in the words of Vatican II, "God orders, directs and governs the entire universe and all the ways of the human community, by a plan conceived in wisdom and love" (Religious Freedom, #3).

The Natural Law: that is, the sharing of the rational creature in the eternal law of God, for, as Vatican II expresses it, "Man has been made by God to participate in this law, with the result that, under the gentle disposition of divine Providence, he can come to perceive ever increasingly the unchanging truth" (Religious Freedom, #3).

The Divine Positive Law: The eternal law of God is manifested in a fuller and clearer way through divine revelation: through "the law and the prophets" in the Old Testament and "in this, the final age, he has spoken to us through his Son" (Hebrews 1:2).

Ecclesiastical (Church) Law: the norms that govern the Church organized as a social and visible structure. See CANON LAW.

Civil Law: usually defined as an ordinance of reason promulgated by authority for the common good; ideally, every civil law should be consistent, just, observable, and useful.

LECTIONARY

A book approved by the Church, containing a three-year cycle of Scripture readings for Sundays and solemn feasts, a two-year weekday cycle, a one-year cycle for the feasts of saints, and readings for ritual Masses and Masses for particular intentions. The present lectionary was approved in 1970; a second edition (substantially the same as the first) was published in 1981. See SACRAMENTARY.

LECTOR

One who reads scriptural and other passages during liturgical worship.

LENT

The penitential season of the Church's year, beginning on Ash Wednesday and ending with the Mass of the Lord's Supper on Holy Thursday; it has six Sundays, the sixth of which is called Passion (Palm) Sunday and marks the beginning of Holy Week. The time of Lent is a penitential time throughout the universal Church; fast and abstinence are to be observed on Ash Wednesday and Good Friday; in the United States, all the Fridays of Lent are days of abstinence from meat. Lent is also a season in which prayer, the reception of the sacraments, charity, and almsgiving are emphasized.

LETTERS (NEW TESTAMENT)

The Letters or Epistles form a large part of the New Testament. These Letters are commonly divided into two general categories: the Pauline Letters and the Catholic Letters. The Pauline Letters were written by Saint Paul himself or by his disciples; they were written not long after the death and Resurrection of Christ (roughly between A.D. 54 and A.D. 80); they are rich firsthand sources of the development of Christian theology and practice. Included in the Pauline Letters are: Romans, 1 Corinthians, 2 Corinthians, Galatians, Ephesians, Philippians, Colossians, 1 Thessalonians, 2 Thessalonians, 1 Timothy, 2 Timothy, Titus, Philemon. (The Letter to the Hebrews is by an unknown author.) The Catholic Letters (so named because they were thought to be addressed not so much to particular communities but to a more general or universal audience) were written by various authors from approximately A.D. 65 to approximately A.D. 95; included in the Catholic Letters are: James, 1 Peter, 2 Peter, 1 John, 2 John, 3 John, Jude, and Revelation.

LIBERTY

See FREEDOM, HUMAN.

LIE

A statement, sign, or action by which one expresses to another something contrary to what one believes to be true, usually with the intention to deceive; speaking against one's interior convictions in order to deceive another. A lie is a violation of the eighth commandment, a perversion of the faculty of speech, and a barrier to mutual trust and confidence in human relationships.

LIMBO
See UNBAPTIZED, FATE OF.

LITURGY
The public worship of the Church, including the celebration of the sacrament and sacrifice of the Eucharist, the celebration of the other sacraments, and the Liturgy of the Hours or the Divine Office (a set form of hymns, psalms, readings, and prayers recited at particular times of the day). Vatican II, in its Constitution on the Sacred Liturgy, teaches that " . . . it is through the liturgy, especially the divine Eucharistic Sacrifice, that 'the work of our redemption is exercised.' The liturgy is thus the outstanding means by which the faithful can express in their lives, and manifest to others, the mystery of Christ and the real nature of the true Church" (#2).

LITURGY OF THE EUCHARIST
See MASS.

LITURGY OF THE WORD
See MASS.

LORD
A customary title for God in the Old Testament; one of the titles given to Jesus in the New Testament, still frequently used in the prayers of the Church (for example, at the beginning — "Lord, Jesus Christ" — or at the conclusion — "through Christ our Lord").

LORD'S DAY
See HOLY DAYS OF OBLIGATION.

LORD'S PRAYER
A term used to describe the prayer that Jesus taught his disciples: see Matthew 6:9-13; used frequently both in the liturgical prayer of the Church and informally by individual Christians; also called the "Our Father."

LOURDES
See SHRINES OF OUR LADY.

LOVE
See CHARITY.

LUKE, GOSPEL OF
One of the four divinely inspired accounts of the life, teaching, death, and Resurrection of Jesus Christ; written around A.D. 80, the author is Luke, a fellow missionary with Saint Paul and also the author of the Acts of the Apostles; his Gospel is directed especially to Gentile Christians, provides many insights into the Christian way of life, emphasizes the compassion and forgiveness of Jesus, and highlights the role of women in the life and ministry of Christ. See ACTS OF THE APOSTLES.

LUST
One of the capital or "deadly" sins, it is the disordered and unrestrained seeking of sexual pleasure.

M

MAGISTERIUM

A Latin word meaning "teaching authority"; according to Catholic doctrine, this teaching authority is vested in the pope, the successor of Saint Peter and the head of the Church, and in the bishops together and in union with the pope. This teaching authority is at times infallible and then demands from the Christian faithful the assent of faith. See INFALLIBILITY.

At other times this teaching authority, though not explicitly infallible, does express authentic Christian Catholic teaching and demands from the Christian faithful the loyal submission of the will and the intellect. Vatican Council II explains the matter in this way: "Bishops, teaching in communion with the Roman Pontiff, are to be respected by all as witnesses to divine and Catholic truth. In matters of faith and morals, the bishops speak in the name of Christ and the faithful are to accept their teaching and adhere to it with a religious assent of soul. This religious submission of will and of mind must be shown in a special way to the authentic teaching authority of the Roman Pontiff, even when he is not speaking ex cathedra. That is, it must be shown in such a way that his supreme magisterium is acknowledged with reverence, the judgments made by him are sincerely adhered to, according to his manifest mind and will. His mind and will in the matter may be known chiefly either from the character of the documents, from his frequent repetition of the same doctrine, or from his manner of speaking" (Dogmatic Constitution on the Church, #25).

MARK, GOSPEL OF

One of the four divinely inspired accounts of the life, teaching, death, and Resurrection of Jesus Christ; the first of the Gospels, and the shortest, it was written around A.D. 65 and was directed especially to Gentile Christians; it provides many details about the ministry and miracles of Jesus, and thus shows that Jesus is the Messiah, the Son of God, and Savior.

MARTYR

From the Greek word for "witness," a martyr is one who voluntarily suffers death for the sake of his or her faith or in defense of some virtue; from the earliest times the Church has held the martyrs in high esteem, honoring their memory and prizing relics of them. See BAPTISM OF BLOOD; RELIC.

MARY, THE BLESSED VIRGIN

Catholic teaching on the Blessed Virgin Mary is extremely rich; only the highlights can be treated here. Mary was the daughter of Joachim and Anne, a native of Nazareth who could trace her lineage to the royal house of David; she was conceived without sin (see IMMACULATE CONCEPTION); she was betrothed to Joseph; she was chosen by God to be the Mother of Jesus (see ANNUNCIATION); she carried this good news to her cousin Elizabeth who greeted her as "the mother of my Lord" and prompted Mary's hymn of praise called the "Magnificat"; she went with Joseph to Bethlehem for a census and there gave birth to Jesus (see VIRGIN BIRTH); in due time she presented Jesus in the temple according to the law, later, she, Joseph, and the Child Jesus fled to Egypt to escape the evil designs of Herod; she and Joseph took Jesus to the temple when he was twelve years old, and there the family became separated for three days. At the beginning of the public ministry of Jesus, Mary was with him at the wedding feast of Cana, where he performed his first miracle; she was at the foot of the Cross when Jesus died; she was present with the apostles in the Upper Room at Pentecost (Acts 1:14); after completing this earthly life, she was assumed body and soul into heaven (see ASSUMPTION OF MARY).

The Church teaches that Mary was conceived without sin, that she remained sinless throughout her life, that she was truly the Mother of God, that she was always a virgin, and that she is able to make intercession for us before God. The Church honors Mary with many liturgical feasts, the most notable being the Immaculate Conception, December 8; the Nativity of Mary, September 8; the Annunciation, March 25; the Purification, February 2; and the Assumption, August 15. The faithful pray to Mary with confidence (see HAIL MARY and ROSARY) and honor her in many ways (see SHRINES OF OUR LADY).

MASS

A popular name for the Eucharistic sacrifice and banquet, the memorial of the death and Resurrection of the Lord, in which the sacrifice of the Lord is perpetuated over the centuries, the summit and source of all Christian worship and life. See EUCHARIST.

The Mass consists of two main parts: the Liturgy of the Word and the Liturgy of the Eucharist. In addition, there are introductory rites (greeting, penitential rite, the Glory to God hymn on certain occasions, opening prayer) and concluding rites (final greeting, blessing, dismissal).

The Liturgy of the Word features the proclamation of the Word of God; on Sundays and other feasts there are three readings (usually including a first reading from the Old Testament, a second reading from the New Testament, and the third reading from one of the Gospels); on other days there are two readings, the final one always from one of the Gospels. Between the readings is a responsorial psalm, and an acclamation is sung before the reading of the Gospel. After the Scripture readings there is a homily on the scriptural or liturgical theme of the Mass with an application to one's Christian life; then follows the Creed on Sundays and other feasts, after which come the general intercessions or prayers of the faithful.

The Liturgy of the Eucharist focuses on the central act of sacrifice in the consecration and on the Eucharistic banquet in Holy Communion. The Liturgy of the Eucharist begins with the presentation of the gifts of bread and wine and prayers of offering by the priest; then follows the Eucharistic Prayer or Canon (see CANON OF THE MASS), the central portion of which is the act of consecration by which the bread and wine are changed into the Body and Blood of Christ. The Eucharistic Prayer closes with a doxology (see DOXOLOGY). The Communion rite begins with a communal praying of the Lord's Prayer, a prayer of deliverance, a prayer for peace and the exchange of some sign of peace, the Lamb of God, and the receiving of Holy Communion by the priest and people, thus completing the sacrifice-banquet of the Mass. A Communion song, period of silence, and prayer after Communion complete the Liturgy of the Eucharist.

MASS, OBLIGATION OF PARTICIPATING IN
See HOLY DAYS OF OBLIGATION.

MATRIMONY, SACRAMENT OF

One of the seven sacraments defined thus by the Church: "The matrimonial covenant, by which a man and a woman establish between themselves a partnership of the whole of life, is by its nature ordered toward the good of the spouses and the procreation and education of offspring; this covenant between baptized persons has been raised by Christ the Lord to the dignity of a sacrament" (Canon 1055, §1). In light of this teaching, the Church emphasizes that "a matrimonial contract cannot validly exist between baptized persons unless it is also a sacrament by that fact" (Canon 1055, §2).

Marriage is marked by two essential properties: "The essential properties of marriage are unity and indissolubility, which in Christian marriage obtain a special firmness in virtue of the sacrament" (Canon 1056).

Marriage is effected by true consent: "Marriage is brought about through the consent of the parties, legitimately manifested between persons who are capable according to law of giving consent; no human power can replace this consent" (Canon 1057, §1). This consent "is an act of the will by which a man and a woman, through an irrevocable covenant, mutually give and accept each other in order to establish marriage" (Canon 1057, §2). Because true consent is so fundamental to the Church's understanding of marriage, there is an entire section of Canon Law dedicated to defining and explaining it (see Canons 1095 to 1107). In brief, this consent must be rational, free, true, and mutual; it can be invalidated by an essential defect, substantial error, the influence of fear or force, or the presence of a condition or intention contrary to the true nature of marriage.

Because marriage is a sacrament, the Church has detailed norms governing the form of its celebration. For Catholics, the basic norm is: "Only those marriages are valid which are contracted in the presence of the local ordinary or the pastor or a priest or deacon delegated by either of them, who assist, and in the presence of two witnesses . . . " (Canon 1108, §1). See ANNULMENT; CONTRACEPTION; DIVORCE; IMPEDIMENTS TO MARRIAGE; MIXED MARRIAGES; NATURAL FAMILY PLANNING.

MATTHEW, GOSPEL OF

One of the four divinely inspired accounts of the life, teaching, death, and Resurrection of Jesus Christ; written in the 70s or 80s A.D., it was directed primarily to Jewish Christians and therefore emphasizes how Jesus is the promised Messiah, the fulfillment of the Old Testament; it gives great attention to the teaching of Jesus by citing many of his discourses and sermons, notably the Sermon on the Mount, chapters 5 through 7.

MEDALS

Metal disks imprinted with the image of Christ, Mary, a saint, or a sacred event. The Church provides a blessing for medals and has long encouraged the use of them as an aid to devotion and prayer; there are a large number of them approved by the Church. At the same time the Church warns against making them objects of superstition. See SACRAMENTALS.

MERCY, CORPORAL AND SPIRITUAL WORKS OF

The corporal works of mercy (flowing from the Gospel, especially Matthew 25:31-46) are: to feed the hungry, give drink to the thirsty, cloth the naked, visit the imprisoned, shelter the homeless, visit the sick, and bury the dead. The spiritual works of mercy, also rooted in the Scriptures, are: to counsel the doubtful, instruct the ignorant, admonish sinners, comfort the afflicted, forgive offenses, bear wrongs patiently, pray for the living and the dead.

MESSIAH

See CHRIST.

MINISTRY

From the word *minister* which means ''to render service''; in the viewpoint of Catholic theology, there is one essential ministry — the ministry of Jesus Christ; his ministry is extended, however, through the members of his Body, the Church. In the Church, the term is used in a variety of ways, among which are the following:

1. Ordained ministry: the service of the People of God by those who have received the sacrament of Holy Orders (that is, bishops, priests, deacons) and who have specific functions de-

termined by the teaching of the Church itself. See BISHOP; PRIEST; DEACON.

2. Nonordained ministry: the service of the People of God undertaken by baptized Catholics either (*a*) with a formal commission from the Church (for example, lector, catechist, acolyte, Eucharistic minister) or (*b*) without a formal commission from the Church (for example, performing the corporal and spiritual works of mercy).

Vatican Council II calls attention to both the variety and the unity of ministries in the Church: ''. . . everyone in the Church does not proceed by the same path, nevertheless all are called to sanctity and have received an equal privilege of faith through the justice of God (see 2 Peter 1:1). And if by the will of Christ some are made teachers, dispensers of mysteries, and shepherds on behalf of others, yet all share a true equality with regard to the dignity and to the activity common to all the faithful for the building up of the Body of Christ'' (Dogmatic Constitution on the Church, #32).

MIRACLES OF CHRIST

The Gospels recount a large number of miracles performed by Jesus Christ: for example, miracles of healing, miracles of raising the dead, and miracles exhibiting control over natural forces. In the New Testament sense, they are signs and wonders — events that are naturally unexplainable — which serve as a motive of credibility by manifesting the power of Christ and inviting those who witness them to faith in Christ himself (see John 2:11).

MISSION

A term used in several different senses, among which are the following:

The Mission of Christ: that is, the exercise of redemptive love, the salvation of the human race: ''The Son of Man has come not to be served but to serve — to give his life in ransom for the many'' (Mark 10:45; see John 16:27-28).

The Mission of the Church: As the Father sent the Son into the world, so the Son sent his apostles and their successors (see John 20:21) into the world to carry on the mission of Christ.

A Mission Territory: a geographical location where the Gospel has not yet been preached or where the response to the Gospel has not yet been sufficient for the local church community there to be considered self-sustaining.

A Parish Mission: a special series of spiritual exercises, with emphasis on the preached word, conducted in a parish to bring about fundamental conversion and renewal of faith among those who attend.

MIXED MARRIAGE

A marriage between a Catholic party and a party who is not Catholic. The basic discipline of the Catholic Church in regard to mixed marriages is explained in the Code of Canon Law: "Without the express permission of the competent authority, marriage is forbidden between two baptized persons, one of whom was baptized in the Catholic Church or received into it after baptism and has not left it by a formal act, and the other of whom is a member of a church or ecclesial community which is not in full communion with the Catholic Church" (Canon 1124). The express permission called for in this Canon may be granted by the local ordinary (bishop) for a just and reasonable cause; according to Canon 1125, he is not to grant this permission, however, unless the following conditions have been fulfilled: "1° the Catholic party declares that he or she is prepared to remove dangers of falling away from the faith and makes a sincere promise to do all in his or her power to have all the children baptized and brought up in the Catholic Church; 2° the other party is to be informed at an appropriate time of these promises which the Catholic party has to make, so that it is clear that the other party is truly aware of the promise and obligation of the Catholic party; 3° both parties are to be instructed on the essential ends and properties of marriage, which are not to be excluded by either party." The Catholic party is bound to the form of marriage (that is, marriage in the presence of the local ordinary [bishop] or the pastor or a priest or deacon delegated by either of them, who assist, and in the presence of two witnesses); but for serious reasons the local ordinary has the right to dispense from the form in individual cases. It is the responsibility of the Catholic party to request this dispensation in due time before the marriage.

MONK

Strictly, a member of one of the monastic orders in the Church, such as Benedictines, Cistercians, Carthusians; popularly, the term is sometimes applied to men who belong to religious communities but who are not monks in the strict sense.

MONSTRANCE

The sacred vessel which holds the consecrated Host when it is exposed for adoration or carried in procession; it is constructed of precious metals and in such a way that the consecrated Host is clearly visible.

MORALITY

In Catholic moral theology, usually defined as the relationship between the human act and the norm of morality; the goodness or badness of a human act deriving from its conformity to or lack of conformity to the norm established by God. The objective norm of morality is especially the eternal law of God, embracing both the natural moral law and the divine positive law. See LAW. The subjective norm of morality is the conscience of the individual person formed in harmony with the divine norm. See CONSCIENCE.

MORTAL SIN

From the Latin word meaning "deadly," the term *mortal* is synonymous in Catholic teaching with "grave" or "serious." A mortal (grave, serious) sin is a personal sin involving a fundamental choice against God in a serious way, a free and willing turning away from his love and law in a grave matter; or, in the words of Saint Thomas Aquinas, "when our acts are so deranged that we turn away from our last end, namely God, to whom we should be united by charity, then the sin is mortal." Traditionally, Catholic theology has emphasized three conditions for mortal sin: (1) that the matter be grave or serious; (2) that there be sufficient reflection or advertence or awareness of the seriousness of the choice one is making; (3) that there be full consent of the will, that is, that one freely chooses to do what one knows is seriously wrong even though one could stop from doing it. According to Catholic teaching, mortal sin brings about the loss of sanctifying grace or friendship with God; grace and friendship are regained especially through the sacrament of Penance, for "Individual and integral confession and absolution constitute the only ordinary way by which the faithful person who is aware of serious sin is reconciled with God and with the Church" (Canon 960). See PENANCE, SACRAMENT OF.

MORTIFICATION

From the Latin word *mors,* which means "death"; the Christian ideal (see Luke 9:23-24 and Galatians 5:24) of "dying to self" through the deliberate restraint of unruly passions and appetites; the struggle against one's evil inclinations so as to bring them into conformity with the will of God. Spiritual writers often distinguish between external mortification (that is, the discipline of the senses by way of fasting, abstinence, control of the tongue, modesty of the eyes) and internal mortification (that is, control over errant passions, emotions, and feelings).

MYSTERY

As used in Catholic theology, a mystery is a divinely revealed truth whose existence cannot be known without revelation by God and whose inner essence cannot be wholly understood by the human mind even after revelation; for example, the mystery of the Trinity, the mystery of the Eucharist. A mystery, in this sense, is said to be above reason but not contrary to reason; even though it cannot be fully understood, it can be understood to some degree, and for that reason the Church encourages all to reflect upon and study the mysteries God has revealed. See THEOLOGY.

MYSTICAL BODY

A term used to describe the Church. Saint Paul speaks of the Church as the Body of Christ; Christ is the Head and we are the members (see Colossians 1:18 and 1 Corinthians 12:27). In 1943 Pope Pius XII wrote a complete encyclical, *The Mystical Body of Christ,* in which he traced this image of the Church through the Christian centuries and in which he concluded: "If we would define and describe the true Church of Jesus Christ — which is the one, holy, catholic, apostolic Roman Church — we shall find nothing more noble, more sublime, or more divine than the expression 'the Mystical Body of Jesus Christ' — an expression that flows spontaneously from the repeated teaching of the sacred Scriptures and the holy Fathers.'' Vatican Council II also explains this image of the Church at length in the Dogmatic Constitution on the Church (#8).

MYSTICISM

An immediate and experiential knowledge of God attained in this present life through religious experiences, especially prayer; it is the fruit of God's freely given grace and results in an intimate union with God as well as a desire to live in his love and to do his will as completely as possible. See CONTEMPLATION.

N

NAME, OF GOD

From a biblical viewpoint, the name signifies more than the external person; it describes also his or her basic personality; thus the name of God signifies God himself. The Israelites held the name of God in such high reverence that they did not even say "Yahweh" but used "Adonai" (the Lord) instead. Likewise, the first Christians held the name Jesus in great reverence (see Philippians 2:9-10). The second commandment inculcates this spirit of reverence: "You shall not take the name of the Lord, your God, in vain. For the Lord will not leave unpunished him who takes his name in vain" (Exodus 20:7). See YAHWEH; JESUS.

NATIONAL CONFERENCE OF CATHOLIC BISHOPS (NCCB)

An ecclesiastical body mandated by Vatican Council II and described thus in the Code of Canon Law: "The conference of bishops, a permanent institution, is a grouping of bishops of a given nation or territory whereby, according to the norm of law, they jointly exercise pastoral functions on behalf of the Christian faithful of their territory in view of promoting that greater good which the Church offers humankind, especially through forms and programs of the apostolate which are fittingly adapted to the circumstances of the time and place" (Canon 447). The National Conference of the American Bishops was established in 1966, has its own bylaws and officers, and meets in plenary session at least annually. The address of the Conference is 1312 Massachusetts Avenue, N.W., Washington, DC 20005. Its service agency is the United States Catholic Conference. See UNITED STATES CATHOLIC CONFERENCE.

NATURAL FAMILY PLANNING

The controlling of conception by limiting the marital act to the infertile periods of the wife. According to Catholic teaching, as expressed by Pope Paul VI, "it is licit to take into account the natural rhythms immanent in the generative functions, for the use of marriage in the infertile periods only, and in this way to regulate birth without offending the moral principles which have been recalled earlier" (*Humanae Vitae,* #16). The methods of natural family planning are constantly being refined; two of the methods widely used are: the sympto-thermal method and the Billings method. See CONTRACEPTION.

NATURAL LAW
The law inherent in the very nature of rational creatures whereby they rightly order their basic conduct with respect to God, others, and themselves. Saint Paul speaks of "the law written in their hearts" (Romans 2:14). Saint Thomas Aquinas defines the natural law as "the participation of the rational creature in the eternal law of God" and argues that all men and women, through the light of reason, are able to arrive at a basic moral code, embracing at least the principle that good must be done and evil avoided. See LAW.

NEW AMERICAN BIBLE
A complete translation of the Bible from the original languages with critical use of all the ancient sources by members of the Catholic Biblical Association of America and sponsored by the Bishops' Committee of the Confraternity of Christian Doctrine; it was begun in 1944 and completed in 1970; it is a translation of the Bible highly respected and widely used by American Catholics and others.

NICENE CREED
A summary of the principal truths of faith that emerged from the Council of Nicea (A.D. 325) and the Council of Constantinople (A.D. 381). It contains a fuller expression of Catholic doctrine, especially on the Holy Trinity, than the Apostles' Creed. The Nicene Creed is the one used in the profession of faith recited after the homily in the Eucharistic liturgy of Sundays and other special feasts.

NON-CHRISTIAN RELIGIONS
Vatican Council II issued a Declaration on the Relation of the Church to Non-Christian Religions; in that Declaration the

Council Fathers referred specifically to the religions of Hindus, Buddhists, Muslims, and especially Jews. According to that Declaration, "The Catholic Church rejects nothing which is true and holy in these religions. She looks with sincere respect upon those ways of conduct and of life, those rules and teachings which, though differing in many particulars from what she holds and sets forth, nevertheless often reflect a ray of that Truth which enlightens all men" (#2). Recognizing that Christians and Jews have "a common spiritual heritage," the Council enouraged "mutual understanding and appreciation" between them. In a summary statement Vatican Council II eloquently insisted that "the Church rejects, as foreign to the mind of Christ, any discrimination against men or harassment of them because of their race, color, condition of life, or religion" (#5). See BUDDHISM; JUDAISM.

NOVENA

A word signifying "nine" and referring to a public or private devotion that extends for nine consecutive days or, in less common usage, for nine consecutive weeks, with the devotion being held on a particular day for those nine weeks. The Church approves of such devotional practices, provided that there is no superstition connected with the number nine and that such externals are used as a help to prayer.

NOVICE

According to the Code of Canon Law, novices are those who begin a period of trial and formation in the novitiate of a religious institute in order to "better recognize their divine vocation" and to "experience the institute's manner of living" (Canon 646). The novice is helped to discern his or her vocation, and is formed both in the essentials of the Christian life and in the charism and spirit of the particular institute. (See Canon 652.) This period must last for 12 months and may be extended to 24 months; at the end of it the novice either leaves or is admitted to temporary vows of poverty, chastity, and obedience. See RELIGIOUS; VOW.

NUN

Popularly, this term is used to describe a woman who belongs to a religious institute, that is, to any "Sister"; technically, the title "nun" applies in the strict sense only to those women who belong to a religious order with solemn vows. See SISTER; VOW.

NUPTIAL MASS

The Mass at which a Catholic is married; it includes a choice of readings, prayers, and blessings that have special relevance to Christian marriage. The nuptial blessing is a formal blessing of the newlywed couple and is given after the Our Father at the nuptial Mass.

O

OATH, TAKING OF
See SWEARING.

OBEDIENCE
The moral virtue which inclines one to submit to the law of God in all of its manifestations, including the eternal law, the natural law, the divine positive law, ecclesiastical law, and civil law. See LAW. Obedience is also one of the evangelical counsels or vows which religious publicly profess in the Church. See RELIGIOUS.

OCCASIONS OF SIN
Extrinsic circumstances (persons, places, or things) which tend to lead one to sin. Theologians make a number of distinctions about occasions of sin, the most important of which are: occasions that are voluntary (that is, of one's own choosing and therefore easily avoidable) and occasions that are necessary (that is, those that cannot easily be avoided); occasions that are proximate (that is, those that frequently lead one to sin) and occasions that are remote (that is, those that seldom lead one to sin.) There is a definite moral obligation to avoid voluntary, proximate occasions of sin; and to take precautions against those that are remote. Most moral theologians hold that to place oneself in a voluntary proximate occasion of sin is itself a sin.

OFFICE, DIVINE
The Liturgy of the Hours; according to Vatican Council II, this is the public prayer of the Church for praising God and sanctifying the day. " . . . the divine Office is arranged so that the whole course of the day and night is made holy by the praises of God. Therefore, when this wonderful song of praise is worthily rendered by priests and others who are deputed for this purpose by

Church ordinance, or by the faithful praying together with the priest in an approved form, then it is truly the voice of the bride addressing her bridegroom; it is the very prayer which Christ Himself, together with His Body, addresses to the Father'' (Constitution on the Sacred Liturgy, #84). See BREVIARY.

OILS, HOLY

A general term for the various kinds of oils used for religious purposes, especially (1) the oil of catechumens used at Baptism; (2) the oil of chrism used at Baptism, at Confirmation, at the ordination of a priest or bishop, in the dedication of churches and altars; and (3) oil of the sick used in anointing the sick. The oils are usually blessed by the bishop at the Mass of Chrism on Holy Thursday (though in cases of necessity they may be blessed at another time or by a priest if the bishop is not available). Traditionally, olive oil has been the oil of preference, but for a good reason the Church allows other oils (from plants, seeds, or coconuts).

OLD TESTAMENT
See BIBLE.

ORDERS, HOLY
See HOLY ORDERS.

ORDERS, RELIGIOUS

A general term commonly used to describe what in the law of the Church are called "institutes of consecrated life"; this consecrated life is thus described in the Code of Canon Law: "Life consecrated by the profession of the evangelical counsels is a stable form of living by which faithful, following Christ more closely under the action of the Holy Spirit, are totally dedicated to God who is loved most of all, so that, having dedicated themselves to His honor, the upbuilding of the Church and the salvation of the world by a new and special title, they strive for the perfection of charity in service to the Kingdom of God and, having become an outstanding sign in the Church, they may foretell the heavenly glory'' (Canon 573, §1). There are in the Church a large number of institutes of consecrated life; they have different purposes and charisms, stemming from the intention of the founders and the different gifts of grace that have been given to them. All of these institutes of consecrated life have goals and norms expressed in their Constitutions and all are in some way under the competent authority of the Church (see Canon 576).

ORGAN TRANSPLANTS

From a moral viewpoint, two types of organ transplants are discussed: (1) the transplant of an organ from a dead person to a living person, for example, a liver transplant; there is no moral objection to this type of transplant, provided of course the donor is truly dead; and (2) the transplant of an organ from one living person to another living person, for example, a kidney transplant; the following norm expresses the Catholic moral position on this type of transplant: ''The transplantation of organs from living donors is morally permissible when the anticipated benefit to the recipient is proportionate to the harm done to the donor, provided that the loss of such organ(s) does not deprive the donor of life itself nor of the functional integrity of his body'' (The Ethical and Religious Directives for Catholic Health Facilities, 30).

ORIGINAL SIN

The sin that occurred at the origin of the human race; the personal sin of Adam, as described in Genesis 2:8—3:24, passed on to all persons (with the certain exception of Jesus Christ and the Blessed Virgin Mary) as a privation of grace; original sin is not a personal sin actually committed by each individual but, rather, in the words of Pope Paul VI, ''It is human nature so fallen, stripped of the grace that clothed it, injured in its natural powers and subjected to the dominion of death, that is transmitted to all men, and it is in this sense that every man is born in sin'' (Credo of the People of God). Original sin means, therefore, that each descendant of Adam is created without sanctifying grace and is subject to concupiscence (that is, the tendency of fallen human nature to act contrary to reason and grace) as well as the punishment of death. Yet human nature is not completely corrupt or incapable of good choices; fallen human nature is capable of receiving sanctifying grace through the death and Resurrection of Jesus Christ (see Romans 5).

ORTHODOX CHURCHES
See EASTERN CHURCHES, SEPARATED.

OUR FATHER
See LORD'S PRAYER.

P

PACIFISM
The moral conviction that all war is intrinsically evil and that it is forbidden by the Gospel; historically, this position (sometimes called "absolute pacifism") has been a minority position among Christians, the more common position being that of the "just war theory"; in recent times, the moral position that opposes not all war but the use of nuclear weapons is sometimes called "relative pacifism." See WAR, MORALITY OF.

PALMS, BLESSED
Palm or other branches blessed and distributed to the faithful on Passion (Palm) Sunday, the sixth Sunday of Lent; the blessed palms are carried in procession to commemorate the triumphant entrance of Jesus into Jerusalem (Matthew 21:1-9) shortly before he died.

PARABLE
A short story drawn from everyday life, used to point out a spiritual lesson; Jesus used parables extensively (more than 30 are recorded in the Gospels) to express some truth about the reign of God (see Matthew 13:11); in reflecting upon parables, the main point — not the particular details — should be especially noted.

PARACLETE
A word meaning "counselor," "defender," or "advocate," it is used in the Gospel of John to refer either to Christ himself, who fulfilled this role for the disciples, or to the Holy Spirit who continues to fulfill this role in the community of the Church (see John 14:16).

PARADISE

A word meaning "garden," with special reference to the Garden of Eden (see Genesis 2:15) and to the eternal abode of the just (Luke 23:43); often used as a synonym for heaven. See HEAVEN.

PARISH

According to the Code of Canon Law, "A parish is a definite community of the Christian faithful established on a stable basis within a particular church; the pastoral care of the parish is entrusted to a pastor as its own shepherd under the authority of the diocesan bishop" (Canon 515, §1). Though a parish is generally territorial, embracing all the faithful within a certain territory, it is also possible that other types of parishes be established "based upon rite, language, the nationality of the Christian faithful within some territory or even upon some other determining factor" (Canon 518). See PASTOR.

PAROUSIA

The second coming of Christ to earth (see 1 Corinthians 15:23), when his triumph over evil will be complete and his kingdom definitively established (see 1 Thessalonians 4:15-17; Luke 24:3-14).

PASCHAL MYSTERY

A phrase referring to the Passion, death, and Resurrection of Jesus Christ, the Lamb of God, by which he brought about salvation for all humankind; also, our way of participating in the dying and rising of Jesus (see 2 Corinthians 4:10-12).

PASSION OF CHRIST

The redemptive sufferings of Jesus as recorded in all four Gospels, featured in a special way during the liturgies of Holy Week. See HOLY WEEK.

PASSOVER

A solemn Jewish feast, celebrated annually on the fifteenth of Nisan (the first month of post-exilic Hebrew calendar, occurring during our March and April), commemorating the deliverance of the Israelites from the bondage of Egypt (see Exodus 12); its main feature was the sacrificial meal, ending with eating the paschal lamb; in later days celebrated in conjunction with the week-long feast of Unleavened Bread. The Christian passover is the sacrifice of Christ, the Lamb of God, by which humankind was freed from the bondage of sin and led into the freedom of the sons and daughters of God.

PASTOR

According to the Code of Canon Law, "The pastor is the proper shepherd of the parish entrusted to him, exercising pastoral care in the community entrusted to him under the authority of the diocesan bishop in whose ministry of Christ he has been called to share; in accord with the norm of law he carries out for his community the duties of teaching, sanctifying and governing, with the cooperation of other presbyters or deacons and the assistance of lay members of the Christian faithful" (Canon 519).

PATROLOGY

The scientific study of the writings of the Fathers of the Church; also called *patristics*. See FATHERS OF THE CHURCH.

PAUL, SAINT

Born in Tarsus around A.D. 5 and originally named Saul; his family were Pharisees, and he was dedicated to persecuting Christians until his extraordinary conversion on the Damascus road (Acts 22:10); having experienced the call of Christ, he dedicated himself with equal fervor to the preaching of the Gospel and became known as the Apostle of the Gentiles during his three major missionary journeys; 13 New Testament Letters bear his name; he was under house arrest for a two-year period and was beheaded outside the city of Rome around A.D. 67; he is buried near the present Roman basilica in honor of Saint Paul; feasts are celebrated in his honor on June 29 (with Saint Peter) and on January 25.

PEACE

A term used among Catholic Christians in several senses, among them: (1) right relationship between God and human beings, a fruit of fidelity to the covenant, a result of reconciliation; (2) right relationships between and among individuals and communities. Christ is the Prince of Peace (see Isaiah 9:5) and came to bring peace (see Luke 2:14) and reconciliation (see Ephesians 2:14-17). True peace can be achieved only by extending the reign of Christ to all human relationships.

PENANCE, SACRAMENT OF
One of the seven sacraments of the Church described thus in the Code of Canon Law: "In the sacrament of penance the faithful, confessing their sins to a legitimate minister, being sorry for them, and at the same time proposing to reform, obtain from God forgiveness of sins committed after baptism through the absolution imparted by the same minister; and they likewise are reconciled with the Church which they have wounded by sinning" (Canon 959).

It is the teaching of the Church that "Individual and integral confession and absolution constitute the only ordinary way by which the faithful person who is aware of serious sin is reconciled with God and with the Church; only physical or moral impossibility excuses the person from confession of this type, in which case reconciliation can take place in other ways" (Canon 960).

Only a priest is the minister of the sacrament of Penance; the priest cannot validly absolve, however, unless he possesses the faculty to do so either from the law of the Church or from competent authority. The confessor acts as both judge and healer in the sacrament of Penance; he is to act with prudence and in fidelity to the magisterium of the Church. The confessor's obligations under the sacramental seal are stated thus: " . . . it is a crime for a confessor in any way to betray a penitent by word or in any manner or for any reason" (Canon 983, §1). See ABSOLUTION; CONTRITION; MORTAL SIN; SEAL OF CONFESSION.

PENTATEUCH
The collective name given to the the first five books of the Bible: namely, Genesis, Exodus, Leviticus, Numbers, and Deuteronomy.

PENTECOST
A liturgical solemnity celebrated 50 days after Easter to commemorate the descent of the Holy Spirit on the apostles and the

baptism of some 3,000 new Christians (see Acts 2:1-41); it is considered "the birthday of the Church," the day of its empowerment to bring the Good News of Jesus Christ to all nations.

PERPETUAL HELP

An ancient and well-loved picture of the Madonna and Child; it is a Byzantine picture and belongs to the "sorrowing" style meant to highlight the meaning of Christ's Passion and death; in the picture, on a background of gold, Mary's head is tilted toward Jesus, her hand loosely clasping his hand; Jesus seems frightened as he gazes into the future; his sandal seems to be falling from his foot; two angels in the upper corners of the picture carry the instruments of Christ's Passion; the original picture was entrusted to the Redemptorists by Pope Pius IX in 1866 and is now enshrined in the Redemptorist Church of San Alfonso in Rome; to honor Mary, the Redemptorists have established the worldwide Archconfraternity of Our Mother of Perpetual Help.

PETER, SAINT

Born in Bethsaida, his name was originally Simon, and he was a fisherman by trade; he was called by Christ, who changed his name to Cephas or Peter or "Rock" and made him the chief of the apostles and the rock on which the Church would be built; he is intimately associated with Jesus in the Gospels and was the first to preach in and around Jerusalem, where he established a Christian community; his name has been traditionally attached to two catholic or general Letters to the Christians in Asia Minor; he established his See in Rome, where he was martyred by crucifixion around A.D. 65 and is buried under what is now St. Peter's Basilica; his feasts are June 29 (with Saint Paul) and February 22.

PHARISEES

A religious sect of the Jews that sought to protect the Jews from contamination by foreign religions and that strove for strict separation from the Gentiles; they insisted on absolute loyalty to the Scriptures and to the traditions of the rabbis; by the time of Christ many (but not all) of the Pharisees had fallen into hypocrisy, and that is why Christ rebuked them so often (see Matthew

23:25; Luke 11:39); they were leaders in the opposition to Christ and his message.

POPE

Also known as the Bishop of Rome, the Vicar of Jesus Christ, the Successor of Saint Peter, the Supreme Pontiff, the Roman Pontiff, his role in the Church is thus described in the Code of Canon Law: "The bishop of the Church of Rome, in whom resides the office given in a special way by the Lord to Peter, first of the Apostles and to be transmitted to his successors, is head of the college of bishops, the Vicar of Christ and Pastor of the universal Church on earth; therefore, in virtue of his office he enjoys supreme, full, immediate and universal ordinary power in the Church, which he can always freely exercise" (Canon 331).

POVERTY

A term used by Christians in several senses, among them: (1) The state of being destitute or in need of the basic necessities of life; this state is opposed to human dignity and is the result of an unjust distribution of the goods of this world, and is seen as a moral and social evil. (2) The state of being "poor in spirit," having the attitude of Christ toward material possessions, that is, seeing them as gifts of God for one's own support, the support of one's family, and the support of those in need. (3) One of the evangelical counsels or vows professed by religious men and women in the Church; it involves the voluntary renunciation of the right to own property or, at least, the renunciation of the independent use and disposal of what one owns, the living of the common life, whereby one gives to the community what one earns and receives from the community what one needs; the details of the vow of poverty are regulated by the Code of Canon Law and by the Constitutions of each religious institute.

PRAYER

An act of the virtue of religion, a response of the intelligent creature to God; among the many definitions or descriptions is the well-known one of Saint Augustine: "Prayer is communication with God"; in the Christian tradition the basic purposes of prayer are to give adoration to God, to thank him for his blessings, to ask pardon for sins, to ask for his grace and help;

there are many forms of prayer, for example: common prayer (with others) and private prayer (alone); common prayer may be liturgical or nonliturgical; private prayer may be vocal or mental. See LITURGY.

PRECEPTS OF THE CHURCH
Obligations imposed on Catholics by the law of the Church; traditionally, six are listed: (1) to participate at Mass on all Sundays and holy days of obligation; (2) to fast and abstain on days designated by the Church; (3) to confess one's sins once a year; (4) to receive Holy Communion during the Easter time; (5) to contribute to the support of the Church; (6) to observe the laws of the Church governing marriage. In 1977 the National Catechetical Directory for Catholics of the United States added two other precepts, namely: ''to study Catholic teaching in preparation for the sacrament of confirmation, to be confirmed, and then to continue to study and advance the cause of Christ'' and ''to join in the missionary spirit and apostolate of the Church.'' All of the traditional precepts of the Church have been reaffirmed in the revised Code of Canon Law, 1983. See ABSTINENCE; EASTER DUTY; FASTING; HOLY DAYS OF OBLIGATION.

PRIDE
One of the capital or ''deadly'' sins, it is a disordered love of self by which one takes personal credit for what are actually gifts of God and by which one seeks unreasonable acclaim for one's accomplishments. See HUMILITY.

PRIEST
A man who through the sacrament of Holy Orders is ordained for the service of the People of God; he has the power to celebrate the Eucharistic sacrifice, to administer the sacraments, to preach the word of God, and to perform pastoral functions according to the mandate of his ecclesiastical superiors. See HOLY ORDERS.

PRIMACY, PAPAL
A charism of the pope as the head of the Church, described in the Code of Canon Law in this way: ''The Roman Pontiff, by virtue of his office, not only has power in the universal Church but also possesses a primacy of ordinary power over all particular

churches and groupings of churches by which the proper, ordinary and immediate power which bishops possess in the particular churches entrusted to their care is both strengthened and safeguarded" (Canon 333, §1).

PROFESSION, RELIGIOUS
The public act by which one embraces the religious state by pronouncing the vows of poverty, chastity, and obedience and promising to live according to the rules and constitutions of a particular religious institute.

PROPAGATION OF THE FAITH
One of the offices of the Roman Curia, technically known as the Sacred Congregation for the Evangelization of Peoples, with special responsibility for all of the Church's missions and missionary efforts throughout the world.

PROPHETS
In the Old Testament, those who wrote or spoke under divine inspiration to make known the will of God or to interpret his message; their message, insofar as it communicated the word of God, related to both their own time and to the future; the prophets of the Old Testament (and the books they wrote) are: Isaiah, Jeremiah, Baruch, Ezekiel, Hosea, Joel, Amos, Obadiah, Jonah, Micah, Nahum, Habakkuk, Zephaniah, Haggai, Zechariah, Malachi.

PRUDENCE
A moral virtue which inclines a person to choose the most suitable means for attaining one's good purposes or for avoiding evil; it demands mature deliberation, taking advice if necessary, a wise judgment, and a right execution of what one has decided.

PSALMS
A collection of 150 songs contained in the Old Testament, expressing thanksgiving, repentance, prophecy, and the spirit of wisdom; though often called "the psalms of David," it is likely that only about half of them were written by David, the others by unknown authors; the Church has long used the Psalms in its liturgical prayer, especially in the Divine Office and at Mass.

PURGATORY

According to Catholic teaching, the state or condition of the elect (that is, those who have died in sanctifying grace or the friendship of God) still in need of purification before they see God; this purification is altogether different from the punishment of the damned. The faithful are encouraged to pray for the souls in purgatory, especially on the feast of All Souls, November 2. See ESCHATOLOGY; ALL SOULS.

PYX

A vessel or container used for carrying the Blessed Sacrament, especially to the sick.

Q

QUIET, PRAYER OF
A form of interior prayer described by Saint Teresa as a spiritual delight in the presence of God, the first step in mystical union with God. See MYSTICISM.

QUIETISM
A form of false mysticism that arose in the seventeenth century, sponsored especially by Michael Molinos, who taught that the human person achieves perfection by complete passivity before God and that once one has submitted to God there is no need to practice virtue, to resist temptation, to participate in the sacraments, or to desire salvation. Quietism was condemned as a heresy by Pope Innocent XI in 1687.

QUMRAN SCROLLS
See DEAD SEA SCROLLS.

R

RACISM
A theory that holds that some human beings are inherently superior and others essentially inferior because of race. From the viewpoint of Catholic moral teaching, as expressed by the American bishops: "Racism is a sin: a sin that divides the human family, blots out the image of God among specific members of that family, and violates the fundamental human dignity of those called to be children of the same Father. . . . It is the sin that makes racial characteristics the determining factor for the exercise of human rights" (*Brothers and Sisters to Us,* 1979).

RAPE
The act of forcing a person, against his or her will, to have sexual intercourse; the force may be physical or moral (for example, fraud or deceit). It is a serious violation of the virtue of justice (violence against the person) as well as of the virtue of chastity.

RASH JUDGMENT
Attributing sins or faults to a person without sufficient reason; unfounded suspicion of another's conduct. It is a violation of justice and charity.

REAL PRESENCE
The teaching of the Church, as defined by the Council of Trent, that "in the sacrament of the most Holy Eucharist is contained truly, really, and substantially the body and blood, together with the soul and divinity, of our Lord Jesus Christ, and consequently the whole Christ." See EUCHARIST.

RECOLLECTION
The practice of being aware of the presence of God or of "walking in the presence of God" so that one may grow in love and fidelity to him.

RECONCILIATION

The act of reestablishing a damaged or destroyed relationship between two parties. Reconciling humankind to God was the primary work of Jesus Christ and is an essential part of the Good News (see 2 Corinthians 4:17-19). According to Catholic teaching, reconciliation with God after one has gravely sinned against him and reconciliation with the Church which is wounded by sin are the basic results of the sacrament of Penance. See PENANCE, SACRAMENT OF.

RECONCILIATION ROOM

A place in most Catholic churches set aside for celebrating the sacrament of Penance; the penitent is given the option of confessing anonymously behind a screen or conversing with the priest face-to-face.

REDEMPTION

Deliverance from sin and restoration of the human race to friendship with God, brought about by the obedient life, saving death, and glorious Resurrection of Jesus Christ, the Redeemer.

REFORMATION, PROTESTANT

A general term that describes the religious upheaval in the Catholic Church in the sixteenth century; some members of the Church, especially Augustinian monk Martin Luther (1483-1546) and John Calvin (1509-1564) opposed abuses in the Church (for example, in regard to indulgences) and challenged some of its basic teachings (for example, concerning original sin, justification, faith) and structure (for example, papal primacy); the result was a serious division within the Catholic community and the birth of Protestant churches. See ECUMENISM.

RELIC

Part of the physical remains of a saint or an object closely associated with a saint; according to Catholic teaching, authentic relics are worthy of veneration by the faithful; the relics of martyrs and other saints are placed in the altar stone of a fixed altar; according to Church law, "it is absolutely forbidden to sell sacred relics" (Canon 1190, §1).

RELIGION

A moral virtue that inclines a person to give due reverence and worship to God as Lord and Creator; the authentic virtue of religion must be both internal (that is, the will or desire to give oneself wholeheartedly to the worship and service of God) and external (that is, the expression of this will or desire through the approved practices of religion — such as prayer, sacrifice, and communal worship). See LITURGY; PRAYER; SACRIFICE.

RELIGIOUS

According to the Code of Canon Law, a person who belongs to a religious institute, that is, "a society in which members, according to proper law, pronounce public vows either perpetual or temporary, which are to be renewed when they have lapsed, and live a life in common as brothers or sisters" (Canon 607, §2). See ORDERS, RELIGIOUS; PROFESSION, RELIGIOUS.

RESTITUTION

Returning to its rightful owner whatever has been unjustly taken from him or her; restoring stolen goods or their equivalent; restitution obliges whenever commutative (person-to-person) justice has been violated; a sin of injustice cannot be forgiven unless the penitent intends to make restitution to the best of his or her ability. See JUSTICE.

RESURRECTION OF CHRIST

The fundamental Christian belief that Jesus Christ arose from the dead (see Mark 16:1-7); it is the cornerstone of the Christian faith, the central theme of apostolic preaching (see 1 Corinthians 15:13-14), the guarantee of the Christians' final resurrection with Christ (see Romans 6:5-8). The Resurrection of Christ is celebrated on the feast of Easter. See EASTER.

RESURRECTION OF THE BODY

The Christian belief (see 1 Corinthians 15:1-58), affirmed in all of the major creeds ("I believe in . . . the resurrection of the body"), that before the Final Judgment each individual soul will be united with its own body and that those who are judged as just will have their bodies glorified.

RETREAT

A special period of prayer, reflection, and solitude for deepening one's relationship with God and renewing one's living of the Christian life; priests and religious are required by Church law to spend some days in retreat each year, and lay people are strongly encouraged to do so.

REVELATION, BOOK OF

The final book of the New Testament, written sometime after A.D. 90 and influenced by Johannine thought; it is a highly symbolic book dealing with things to come and the struggle between the Church and the powers of evil; though it contains dire warnings, it is fundamentally a message of hope to the Church concerning the final triumph of the Lord Jesus Christ.

REVELATION, DIVINE

The manifestation of God and his plan of salvation to humankind; in Catholic theology, a distinction is sometimes made between the body of revealed truth given to us by God ("divine revelation") and the process by which he has revealed it, especially through his Son, Jesus Christ, who in the words of Vatican II "perfected revelation" and "confirmed with divine testimony what revelation proclaimed. . . ." (Divine Revelation, #4); this revelation of God is found in the community of believers which is the Church, whose primary function, especially through its magisterium or teaching office, is to preserve it intact and hand it on to each new generation. See BIBLE; MAGISTERIUM; TRADITION.

RIGHTS, HUMAN

According to Catholic social teaching, each human person is endowed by God with certain fundamental and inalienable rights; perhaps the most complete enumeration and explanation of these rights is contained in Pope John XXIII's encyclical *Peace on Earth* (*Pacem in Terris*, 1963, especially #14 to #27); among the more important listed are: the right to life, to bodily integrity, to the means necessary for the development of life, to security in sickness or old age, to respect for one's person and good reputation, to a share in the benefits of one's culture, to the free exercise of religion, to freedom of choice in regard to one's state in life, to a just wage, to safe working conditions, to the ownership of private property, to freedom of assembly and association, to freedom of movement (emigration and immigration), to an active part in public affairs, and to just juridical protection.

RITES

A term used to describe the forms and ceremonies in liturgical worship; the words and actions that belong to a religious ceremony, for example, the rite of Baptism. The term is used also to group various communities within the Catholic Church in accordance with their official ritual usages, for example, Roman Rite Catholics and Byzantine Rite Catholics. See EASTERN CHURCHES, CATHOLIC.

ROSARY

A popular devotion among Catholics, including meditation on the main mysteries of salvation as well as the recitation of certain vocal prayers. The mysteries are divided into three groups of five as follows: The Joyful Mysteries (the Annunciation, the Visitation, the Nativity, the Presentation in the Temple, the Finding in the Temple); the Sorrowful Mysteries (the Agony in the Garden, the Scourging, the Crowning with Thorns, the Carrying of the Cross, the Crucifixion); the Glorious Mysteries (the Resurrection, the Ascension, the Descent of the Holy Spirit, the Assumption of Mary into Heaven, the Coronation of Mary). Meditation on each mystery is accompanied by the vocal praying of one Our Father, ten Hail Marys, and one Glory Be. To help the praying of the rosary, a string of beads (a "rosary") is usually used. The Church strongly recommends the praying of the rosary, especially the family rosary.

S

SABBATH
The seventh day of the week (Saturday), prescribed in the Decalogue as a day to be kept holy, a day of rest and religious observance (see Deuteronomy 5:12-14), held in special reverence by religious Jews; the manner of observing it became a source of conflict between Jesus and the Pharisees (see Mark 2:27); in apostolic times Christians transferred the Sabbath to the first day of the week in honor of the Resurrection of Christ and called it "the Lord's Day." See HOLY DAYS OF OBLIGATION.

SACRAMENTALS
The Church's understanding of the sacramentals is thus described in the Code of Canon Law: "Somewhat in imitation of the sacraments, sacramentals are sacred signs by which spiritual effects especially are signified and are obtained by the intercession of the Church" (Canon 1166). Some well-known sacramentals are blessings by a priest, blessed palms, blessed candles, blessed medals and scapulars, holy water.

SACRAMENTARY
A part of the Roman Missal containing the prayers and directives (but not the Scripture readings) for the celebration of Mass and a number of sacramental formulas; it was revised in accord with the principles of Vatican II and approved by the Church in 1970. See LECTIONARY.

SACRAMENTS
The Church's understanding of the sacraments, which are seven in number, is thus described in the Code of Canon Law: "The sacraments of the New Testament, instituted by Christ the Lord and entrusted to the Church, as they are the actions of Christ and the Church, stand out as the signs and means by which the faith is expressed and strengthened, worship is rendered to God and the

sanctification of humankind is effected, and they thus contribute in the highest degree to the establishment, strengthening and manifestation of ecclesial communion; therefore both the sacred ministers and the rest of the Christian faithful must employ the greatest reverence and the necessary diligence in their celebration'' (Canon 840). See BAPTISM; CONFIRMATION; EUCHARIST; PENANCE; HOLY ORDERS; MARRIAGE, CHRISTIAN; ANOINTING OF THE SICK.

SACRED HEART OF JESUS
The physical heart of Jesus as a sign and symbol of his immense love for human beings for whom he accomplished the work of redemption; the Church celebrates the solemnity of the Sacred Heart on the Friday after the second Sunday after Pentecost; the Church encourages the faithful to practice approved devotion in honor of the Sacred Heart.

SACRED SCRIPTURE
See BIBLE.

SACRIFICE
From a religious viewpoint, the form of worship by which a duly authorized minister offers a victim in recognition of God's supreme dominion; in the Old Testament true and authentic sacrifices were offered, but they were imperfect ''because it is impossible for the blood of bulls and goats to take sins away'' (Hebrews 10:4); in the New Testament Christ himself is the perfect sacrifice, who with his own blood ''achieved eternal redemption'' (Hebrews 9:12). The sacrifice of Christ is perpetuated in the Eucharist. See EUCHARIST.

SACRILEGE
A violation or contemptuous treatment of a person, place, or thing that is publicly dedicated to the worship of God; in essence it amounts to a personal affront against God.

SACRISTY
A room annexed to a church used to store sacred vessels and other materials used in the liturgy, and to provide a place for priests and other ministers to vest and prepare for liturgical celebrations.

SAINT

In the wide sense, any person known for Christian holiness; in the strict sense, a person who has manifested heroic virtue during his or her life and who is officially honored by the Church as one who has attained heavenly glory and as one through whom God freely chooses to exhibit exceptional generosity. See CANONIZATION.

SAINTS, VENERATION OF

The ancient tradition of honoring and invoking the saints, explained by Vatican II in this way: "The Church has always believed that the apostles, and Christ's martyrs who had given the supreme witness of faith and charity by the shedding of their blood, are quite closely joined with us in Christ. She has always venerated them with special devotion, together with the Blessed Virgin Mary and the holy angels. The Church too has devoutly implored the aid of their intercession . . ." (Dogmatic Constitution on the Church, #50).

SALVATION

Deliverance from sin and eternal union with God in heaven made possible by the paschal mystery of Jesus Christ, Lord and Savior, and by its fruits offered in the Church, especially through the sacraments.

SANCTIFYING GRACE

According to Catholic teaching, a created participation or sharing in the life of God himself; friendship with God. See GRACE.

SATAN

See DEVIL.

SCANDAL

An action, word, or omission which has at least the appearance of evil and is likely to lead another into sin; there is a distinction between direct scandal (that is, one person deliberately intends to lead another into sin) and indirect scandal (that is, one person foresees that his or her action or omission may lead another into sin but does not deliberately intend this). Direct scandal is always morally evil; indirect scandal may sometimes be permitted when one's actions are morally good and there is sufficient reason to allow the evil effect.

SCAPULAR

An outer garment worn by members of some religious orders, consisting of a shoulder-wide strip of cloth reaching almost to the floor in front and back and symbolizing the yoke of Christ; also an adaptation of this (two small pieces of cloth connected by strings) worn around the neck by persons who do not belong to the religious order; a scapular approved by the Church is a sacramental. See SACRAMENTALS.

SCRUPULOSITY

A religious-moral-psychological state of more or less severe anxiety, fear, and indecision; an unreasonable and morbid fear of sin, error, and guilt.

SEAL OF CONFESSION

The secrecy demanded of the confessor in the sacrament of Penance; no reason whatever justifies the breaking of this seal, and the Church reserves grave penalties for any confessor who would dare to do so (see Canon 1388).

SECOND COMING

See PAROUSIA.

SECULAR CLERGY

See CLERGY.

SECULAR INSTITUTE

According to the Code of Canon Law, "A secular institute is an institute of consecrated life in which the Christian faithful living in the world strive for the perfection of charity and work for the sanctification of the world especially from within" (Canon 710). Persons who belong to an institute of consecrated life profess the evangelical counsels of chastity, poverty, and obedience according to the constitutions of their particular institute (see Canon 573).

SECULARISM

A philosophy of life that in theory or practice rejects the value of the supernatural in human life; it professes that human existence and destiny belong to this world only, with no reference to eternal realities.

SELF-DEFENSE
The moral right to use force against an unjust aggressor.

SEMINARY
A place where candidates for the priesthood (called seminarians) pursue their academic, apostolic, and spiritual formation.

SERMON ON THE MOUNT
The comprehensive presentation of the teachings of Jesus as presented in the Gospel of Matthew, chapters 5, 6, 7; a briefer version is found in the Gospel of Luke 6:20-49; it has been called the "*Magna Charta* of Christianity" and contains the teaching of Jesus on true discipleship, including an explanation of the Beatitudes, the Lord's Prayer, and the relationship of the old law to the new law in Christ.

SEX EDUCATION
Instruction in the fundamental meaning of human sexuality and the right use of sex according to one's state in life; the Church has often spoken in favor of proper sex education and has given guidelines for it, the most recent document being *Educational Guidance in Human Love: Outlines of Sex Education* issued by the Vatican Congregation for Catholic Education in December 1983.

SHRINES OF OUR LADY
Holy places where apparitions of the Blessed Virgin Mary are believed to have taken place; because of their reputation as places where moral and physical miracles have been granted, they are centers of pilgrimages; among the outstanding shrines of the Blessed Virgin Mary the following four (in alphabetical order) are especially noteworthy:

1. Fatima, Portugal: Between May 13 and October 13, 1917, Mary appeared six times to three children near Fatima, north of Lisbon. After intense study, Church authorities pronounced these apparitions worthy of belief in 1930. The message of Mary at Fatima included an exhortation to frequent recitation of the rosary, works of mortification on behalf of sinners, the con-

secration of the people of Russia to her under the title of her Immaculate Heart, and the observance of the first Saturday of each month by receiving Holy Communion in reparation for sin.

2. Guadalupe, Mexico: In 1531 Mary appeared four times to Juan Diego on Tepeyac Hill near Mexico City; a life-size figure of Mary was miraculously painted on Juan Diego's mantle; this painting is now enshrined in the basilica at the shrine; the Church has accepted the apparition as authentic and celebrates the feast of Our Lady of Guadalupe (the "Mother of the Americas") on December 12.

3. La Salette, France: In September 1846, Mary appeared to two peasant children; in 1851 Church authorities declared the apparition worthy of belief, and devotion to Our Lady of La Salette was approved. The chief message of our Lady was the necessity of penance on the part of the faithful.

4. Lourdes, France: Between February and July, 1858, Mary (identifying herself by saying, "I am the Immaculate Conception") appeared 18 times to a young woman, Bernadette Soubirous. After four years of intense study, Church authorities approved the apparitions as authentic in 1862. Mary's message was a solemn exhortation to prayer and penance for the conversion of peoples. The feast of Our Lady of Lourdes is celebrated on February 11.

SHROUD OF TURIN
A linen cloth bearing on front and back the imprint of a human body; a tradition of some antiquity holds that the shroud is actually the burial cloth in which Jesus was wrapped after his death; scientific research has been conducted in this century and seems to uphold the view that the shroud bears the marks of a human body that was scourged, crowned with thorns, and crucified; the Church has never made a pronouncement about the authenticity of the shroud, but many Christians consider it a holy relic of the death of Christ.

SIGN OF THE CROSS
A gesture in the form of a cross by which one professes his or her faith in the holy Trinity; it is made in several ways: (1) one

"blesses oneself," for example, at the beginning and end of one's prayers, by touching the fingers of one's right hand to one's forehead, breast, left shoulder, and right shoulder while saying, "In the name of the Father, and of the Son, and of the Holy Spirit"; (2) one forms a small cross on one's forehead, lips, and breast before the proclamation of the Gospel; (3) one authorized to give blessings in the Church makes a large cross with one's right hand over the person or object to be blessed. See BLESSING.

SIMONY
Intentional buying or selling of something spiritual (for example, grace, a sacrament) or something closely connected with the spiritual (for example, a relic); both the law of God and the law of the Church forbid such buying and selling because it is a violation of the honor due to God and the things of God. See SACRILEGE.

SIN
In Catholic theology, a term used to describe two separate realities: original sin and actual sin. Original sin is the sin of Adam that brought about evil effects on the human race; see ORIGINAL SIN. Actual (or personal) sin is a fundamental choice against God, a free and willing turning away from his love and his law. Actual sin may be either mortal or venial. See MORTAL SIN; VENIAL SIN.

SISTER
Popularly, a title given to any woman who belongs to a religious institute; strictly, the title belongs to a woman who belongs to a religious institute that professes simple, not solemn, vows. See NUN; VOW.

SLANDER
See CALUMNY.

SLOTH
One of the capital or "deadly" sins, it is a kind of spiritual laziness or boredom in regard to the things of God, frequently leading to neglect of one's spiritual duties.

SOCIAL JUSTICE

A part of the cardinal virtue of justice; according to Catholic social teaching, it is that aspect of justice which urges the individual member of a social group to seek the common good of the whole group rather than just his or her own individual good; it presumes, in the explanation of Pope Pius XII, a "social conscience that calls individuals to their social duties, urges them to take into account in all their activities their membership in a community, to be preoccupied with the welfare of their neighbors and with the common good of society." Social justice strives to bring authentic moral values to the organization of society and to the social institutions (educational, economic, political) by which society functions. See UNIONS, LABOR; WAGE, JUST; WORK.

SOUL

That part of the human person that animates the body; the principle of spiritual activities such as thinking and willing; according to Catholic teaching, the human soul is individually created for each person by God and infused at the time of conception and is immortal.

SPIRITISM

Also called spiritualism, it is the belief that the living can communicate with spirits and with the deceased by way of a human medium or inanimate objects, such as a Ouija board; practices derived therefrom are a violation of the first commandment of the Decalogue and opposed to the virtue of religion.

SPIRITUAL EXERCISES

See RETREAT.

SPIRITUAL LIFE

A term used by Christians to refer to the interior life of sanctifying grace, by which one shares in the life of the triune God (see John 14:23) and becomes a temple of the Holy Spirit, and to describe the efforts of the individual Christian to cultivate that life by participating in the sacraments, prayer, works of penance and charity.

SPIRITUAL WORKS OF MERCY
See MERCY, CORPORAL AND SPIRITUAL WORKS OF.

SPONSOR
See BAPTISMAL SPONSOR; CONFIRMATION, SACRAMENT OF.

STATIONS OF THE CROSS
See WAY OF THE CROSS.

STERILITY
The inability to generate children because of some physical defect; according to the Code of Canon Law, "Sterility neither prohibits nor invalidates marriage" (Canon 1084, §3). See IMPOTENCE.

STERILIZATION
Depriving a person of the reproductive function; according to Catholic moral teaching, it is morally justified when necessary for life or health; but as a contraceptive measure it is a grave violation of the moral law. See CONTRACEPTION.

STEWARDSHIP
The religious conviction that every gift of nature and grace comes from God and that the human person is not the absolute master of his or her gifts and possessions but, rather, the trustee (steward) of them (see 1 Peter 4:10); they are given "in trust" for the building up of the kingdom of God.

STIPEND, MASS
An offering made to a priest on the occasion of requesting a Mass to be offered for one's personal intentions; according to the Code of Canon Law, "In accord with the approved usage of the Church, it is lawful for any priest who celebrates or concelebrates Mass to receive an offering to apply the Mass according to a definite intention" (Canon 945, §1), but at the same time priests are urged to "celebrate Mass for the intention of the Christian faithful, especially of the needy, even if no offering has been received" (Canon 945, §2); the faithful who make such an offering "contribute to the good of the Church and by their offering take part in the concern of the Church for the support of

its ministers and works'' (Canon 946); the Code of Canon Law also insists that ''Any appearance of trafficking or commerce is to be entirely excluded from Mass offerings'' (Canon 947) and has strict regulations governing this entire matter (see Canons 948-958).

STOLE
See VESTMENTS.

STRIKE
An organized work stoppage on the part of employees for the purpose of obtaining values or benefits that employees believe they are entitled to; according to Catholic social teaching, a strike is morally justified provided that there is a just cause for it, that there is proper authorization by a free decision of the employees or those who represent them, that it is a last resort (after every other reasonable means has been exhausted), and that only just means are used in carrying it out.

SUICIDE
Intentionally causing one's own death; objectively speaking, suicide is a serious violation of God's law, a rejection of God's sovereignty and loving plan; subjectively, however, suicide often seems to result from profound psychological disturbances or mental imbalances and thus may not be the result of a free and deliberate human act.

SUNDAY
See HOLY DAYS OF OBLIGATION.

SUPERSTITION
Either the worship of God in an unworthy manner (for example, by bizarre cultic practices) or attributing to persons or objects a power which belongs to God alone (for example, astrology, spiritism); superstition is a violation of true religion.

SUPPORT OF CHURCH
One of the precepts or commandments of the Church rooted in the biblical principle of stewardship and based on the fact that the Church, in both its local and worldwide dimensions, depends

upon the voluntary contributions of the faithful to carry on its ministry. See STEWARDSHIP.

SWEARING
Calling on the name of God to witness to the truth of a statement or promise; according to Catholic teaching, swearing is justified only in support of the truth and in favor of justice.

SYNAGOGUE
The Jewish meeting place or center, less sacred and formal than the temple, used for religious worship, biblical readings and study, prayer, and other community affairs.

SYNOD OF BISHOPS
According to the Code of Canon Law, "The synod of bishops is that group of bishops who have been chosen from different regions of the world and who meet at stated times to foster a closer unity between the Roman Pontiff and the bishops, to assist the Roman Pontiff with their counsel in safeguarding and increasing faith and morals and in preserving and strengthening ecclesiastical discipline, and to consider questions concerning the Church's activity in the world" (Canon 342).

SYNOPTIC GOSPELS
Synoptic is from a Greek word meaning "seeing the whole together" and is applied to the Gospels of Matthew, Mark, and Luke because they present a similar view of the life and teaching of Jesus. See GOSPEL.

T

TABERNACLE

A receptacle for the exclusive reservation of the Most Holy Eucharist; according to the Code of Canon Law, it "should be placed in a part of the church that is prominent, conspicuous, beautifully decorated, and suitable for prayer" (Canon 938, §2); moreover, it should be "immovable, made of solid and opaque material, and locked so that the danger of profanation may be entirely avoided" (Canon 938, §3); a special lamp (often called the sanctuary lamp) "to indicate and honor the presence of Christ is to burn at all times before the tabernacle in which the Most Holy Eucharist is reserved" (Canon 940).

TALMUD

The Jewish compilation containing the Mishnah or oral interpretations of the law in written form; many Jews (and Christians too) still consider it an authoritative guide and aid to the spiritual life.

TEACHING OFFICE OF THE CHURCH

See MAGISTERIUM.

TEMPERANCE

One of the cardinal virtues; it moderates and regulates the desire for pleasure, especially but not exclusively in regard to the pleasures of eating, drinking, and sex.

TEMPORAL PUNISHMENT

The punishment still due to venial or mortal sins already forgiven; it is "temporal" as opposed to "eternal," that is, the punishment of hell; temporal punishment may be remitted in this life by the practice of penance and other virtues, in the next life by suffering in purgatory. See INDULGENCE; PURGATORY.

TEMPTATION

An attraction or enticement to sin, arising from within a person or from without (that is, "from the world, the flesh, or the devil"); it is not of itself a sin but an opportunity or occasion of proving one's fidelity to God; Catholic moral teaching encourages the Christian to deal with temptation by prayer for grace and prudent action.

TESTAMENT

See COVENANT.

THEFT

The secret taking of another's goods against his or her reasonable wishes; it is a sin against the seventh commandment, a violation of commutative (person-to-person) justice.

THEOLOGICAL VIRTUES

The three virtues of faith, hope, and charity that are God-given (infused with the gift of sanctifying grace) and God-directed (that is, God himself is their direct object); these virtues enable us to know and love God in himself and lead to union with him in mind and heart. See FAITH; HOPE; CHARITY.

THEOLOGY

The science that treats of God, the things that relate to God, and God's relations with the world; it is, according to an ancient definition, "faith seeking understanding," that is, a systematized and organized study of what God has revealed and what believers have accepted; this science has historically been divided into a number of branches, such as dogmatic theology, moral theology, pastoral theology, etc.

THOMAS AQUINAS, SAINT

Born in Italy around 1225, he joined the Order of Preachers (Dominicans) and became one of the greatest theologians in the history of the Church; his genius was the ability to relate faith and reason, theology and philosophy; he wrote many works, the chief of which was his *Summa Theologica*, a broad exposition of theology as related to philosophical principles; he died in 1274, was canonized in 1323; he is considered one of the greatest Doctors of the Church and a sure guide in Catholic theology.

TITHING
The biblical mandate that one should contribute one-tenth of one's income to support the works of religion and charity; sometimes used to describe any fixed pledge of income, even if less than one-tenth.

TORAH
A term commonly used to refer to the Mosaic Law as contained in the Pentateuch or first five books of the Bible, namely, Genesis, Exodus, Leviticus, Numbers, and Deuteronomy.

TRADITION
According to Catholic teaching, one of the sources (together with Sacred Scripture) of divine revelation; it is, in the words of Vatican II, "the Word of God which has been entrusted to the apostles by Christ the Lord and the Holy Spirit"; unlike many Christian communities that teach that Scripture alone is the source of divine revelation, the Catholic Church professes that "Sacred tradition and sacred scripture form one sacred deposit of the word of God, which is committed to the Church" (Divine Revelation, #10).

TRANSFIGURATION OF CHRIST
The appearance in glory of Jesus Christ during his earthly life, as recorded in Matthew 17:1-13, Mark 9:2-13, and Luke 9:28-36; a significant event that showed the Lord to be the Messiah, reaffirmed his sonship with the Father, and foreshadowed his future glory; this event is commemorated on the second Sunday of Lent each year, and there is a special feast of the Transfiguration on August 6.

TRANSUBSTANTIATION
In Catholic theology of the Eucharist, a technical term that describes the change of the whole substance of bread and wine into the whole substance of the Body and Blood of Christ while only the accidents or appearances (taste, smell, etc.) of bread and wine remain.

TRENT, COUNCIL OF
The nineteenth ecumenical council of the Catholic Church held in 25 sessions between 1545 and 1563; its primary work was a defense of Catholic teaching against the attacks of the Protestant reformers; in presenting this defense it also offered a comprehensive treatment of Christian teaching on the nature of justification, original sin, grace, faith, the seven sacraments (especially the Eucharist), the veneration of saints, purgatory, and indulgences. Trent set in motion a number of Catholic reforms in regard to the liturgy, the religious education of the faithful, the training of candidates for the priesthood, and the devotional life of the Church. Its influence was, for the most part, widespread and positive, and it is considered one of the most important of the Church's ecumenical councils.

TRIDUUM
A three-day series of public or private devotions, similar to a novena except for the shorter time period. See NOVENA.

TRINITY, HOLY
See HOLY TRINITY.

U

UNBAPTIZED, FATE OF

If, as the Church professes, Baptism is necessary for salvation (see John 3:5), what can be said of the salvation of those who die without Baptism? This theological question has been pondered for centuries. Briefly, Catholic teaching holds that, in the case of adults, there are two possibilities: (1) Baptism of blood or martyrdom (see BAPTISM OF BLOOD) and (2) Baptism of desire (see BAPTISM OF DESIRE). In the case of infants, a rather common theological opinion has been that infants who die without Baptism are excluded from heaven but spend eternity in a state of natural happiness called limbo. This theological explanation has never been explicitly taught by the Church. Another fairly common theological explanation has been that God in his mercy can supply for the lack of Baptism in a way that has not been revealed to us. In a document from the Vatican's Congregation of the Faith (1980), it is said that the Church "knows no other way apart from Baptism for ensuring children's entry into eternal happiness"; but in regard to children who die without Baptism, the Church "can only entrust them to the mercy of God, as she does in the funeral rite provided for them."

UNIONS, LABOR

Catholic social teaching has long defended the right of workers to form associations to protect their vital interests, while at the same time insisting that unions should pursue their goals only in morally acceptable ways. The most recent authoritative statement of these principles is to be found in the encyclical letter of Pope John Paul II, *On Human Work* (*Laborem Exercens*), especially #20. After discussing various rights of workers within the context of basic human rights, the pope points out: "All these rights, together with the need for workers to secure them, give rise to yet another right: the right of association, that is, to form associations for the purpose of defending the vital interests of those employed in the various professions. These associations are called labor or trade unions. . . . " These unions should always strive "to secure the just rights of workers within the framework of the common good of the whole of society. . . . "

UNITED STATES CATHOLIC CONFERENCE (USCC)
A service agency for the National Conference of Catholic Bishops; its purpose, as described in *The Official Catholic Directory,* is to assist "the Bishops in their service to the Church in this country by uniting the people of God where voluntary collective action on a broad interdiocesan level is needed" and to provide "an organizational structure and the resources needed to insure coordination, cooperation, and assistance in the public educational, and social concerns of the Church at the national or interdiocesan level."

URBI ET ORBI
Literally, this phrase means "to the city and the world"; specifically, it refers to the solemn blessing of the pope given to his visible audience in the city of Rome and also to the entire invisible audience of the faithful throughout the world.

USURY
In moral theology, the taking of excessive or exorbitant interest on the loan of money. It is a violation of the virtue of justice.

V

VALIDATION OF MARRIAGE

The making valid of a marriage contract that was originally invalid for one of three reasons: (1) because of the presence of a diriment (invalidating) impediment; (2) because of a defect of consent; (3) because of a defect of form. The procedures for validation in these cases are given in the Code of Canon Law, Canon 1156 through Canon 1160. See IMPEDIMENTS TO MARRIAGE; MATRIMONY, SACRAMENT OF.

VATICAN COUNCIL I

The twentieth ecumenical (general) council of the Catholic Church held in Rome during the pontificate of Pope Pius IX, from December 1, 1869, to October 20, 1870. This council dealt at length with questions regarding faith, revelation, and the relationship between faith and reason; it is best known for its definition on the universal jurisdictional primacy of the pope and his infallibility when proclaiming by a definitive act some doctrine of faith or morals. See INFALLIBILITY.

VATICAN COUNCIL II

The twenty-first ecumenical council of the Catholic Church held in Rome in four sessions: the first during the pontificate of Pope John XXIII, October 11 to December 8, 1962; the other three during the pontificate of Pope Paul VI, September 29 to December 4, 1963, September 14 to November 21, 1964, and September 14 to December 8, 1965. This was the largest (2,800 members) and most productive (16 significant documents) of all the ecumenical councils. The teaching of Vatican II had an enormous impact on the Church in all parts of the world. Of the 16 documents enacted by the council 4 were constitutions of major importance for the whole Church, 9 were decrees on particular topics or for particular groups within the Church, and 3 were declarations. Space permits only a brief description of each of these documents:

• The Dogmatic Constitution on the Church sets forth the Church's understanding of her own nature. Its first chapter, "The Mystery of the Church," presents the vision of the Church at once divine and human, embracing all people of good will, namely "the People of God" (second chapter). The third chapter describes the bishops of the world as a "college" collectively responsible, under the leadership of the pope, for the work of the Church. The fourth chapter deals in a very positive way with the role of the laity in the Church; the fifth with the universal call to holiness; the sixth with religious communities; the seventh with the relationship between the pilgrim Church on earth and the "Heavenly Church." Chapter eight, the final chapter, pertains to the role of the Blessed Virgin Mary.

• The Dogmatic Constitution on Divine Revelation sets forth the Church's teaching on how God reveals himself to humankind. The transmission of this revelation is recorded in written form in the Scriptures; its transmission by word of mouth is part of the tradition of the Church. Both Scripture and tradition spring from one and the same source.

• The Constitution on the Sacred Liturgy sets forth the Church's teaching on worship as the heart of her life. It instructed that the sacred texts and rites should be drawn up so that they express more clearly the holy things which they signify and that the Christian people, as far as possible, should be able to understand them with ease and take part in them fully, actively, and as befits a community.

• The Pastoral Constitution on the Church in the Modern World sets forth the Church's sincere effort to speak to all men and women to shed light on the dignity of the human person and to cooperate in finding solutions to the outstanding problems of our time.

• The nine decrees addressed the following subjects: the pastoral office of bishops, ecumenism, the Oriental Catholic Churches, the ministry and life of priests, education for the priesthood, the renewal of religious life, the missionary activity of the Church, the apostolate of the laity, and the instruments of social communication.

• The three declarations dealt with religious freedom, the Church's attitude toward non-Christians, and Christian education.

VATICAN, THE

A name used to describe a number of different realities: for example, the residence of the pope built upon the Vatican Hill in the city of Rome; the various congregations or tribunals through which the pope governs the Church; the basilica of Saint Peter; the sovereign state of 109 acres, established in 1929 by an agreement between the pope and the Italian government, ruled as an independent territory by the pope.

VENIAL SIN

In contrast to mortal (grave, serious) sin, a venial sin may be described as a less serious rejection of God's love, not a fundamental choice against God, not a complete turning away from him. It is a failure to love God and others as much as we should, a transient neglect of God and his law. Saint Thomas describes it this way: "Although a person who commits a venial sin does not actually refer his or her act to God, nevertheless he or she still keeps God as his or her habitual end. The person does not decisively set himself or herself on turning away from God, but from overfondness for a created good falls short of God. He or she is like a person who loiters, but without leaving the way."

VESTMENTS

Garments used in the celebration of the Eucharistic liturgy and other sacraments. The vestments have their origin in the ordinary dress of the Roman Empire in the first centuries of Christianity, but they have taken on a symbolic meaning also. The principal vestments now in use are:

Amice: a square or oblong piece of linen (or similar material) to which two long tapes are attached at the upper corners. It is worn over the shoulders and is symbolic of "the helmet of salvation."

Alb: a long, white (*albus* is Latin for white) garment, symbolic of the total purity that should cover one in one's approach to God.

Cincture: a cord worn around the waist to keep the alb neatly in place.

Stole: a long, thin band of appropriate material worn around the neck and shoulders, symbolic of the "yoke of the Lord"; it is worn by the priest in the solemn celebration of all the sacraments (the deacon wearing it over the shoulder only).

Chasuble: The outermost garment worn by the priest in the celebration of Mass.

VIATICUM

The reception of Holy Communion when there is probable danger of death. According to Canon Law: "The Christian faithful who are in danger of death, arising from any cause, are to be nourished by Holy Communion in the form of Viaticum" (Canon 921). It is important that Viaticum not be delayed too long but that the sick be nourished with this "food for the journey" while they are still conscious.

VIRGIN BIRTH

The basic Christian doctrine that Jesus Christ was conceived and born of Mary while she remained a virgin; this belief is included in all the creeds ("I believe in Jesus Christ, his only Son, who was born of the virgin Mary . . . ") and is an article of Catholic faith.

VIRGINITY

The observance of perpetual sexual abstinence. In the Christian context its motive is "for the sake of God's reign" (Matthew 19:12). In speaking of the evangelical counsels, Vatican II teaches that "Outstanding among them is that precious gift of divine grace which the Father gives to some men (see Matthew 19:11; 1 Corinthians 7:7) so that by virginity, or celibacy, they can more easily devote their entire selves to God alone with undivided heart (see 1 Corinthians 7:32-34). This total continence embraced on behalf of the kingdom of heaven has always been held in particular honor by the Church as being a sign of charity and stimulus towards it, as well as a unique fountain of spiritual fertility in the world'' (Dogmatic Constitution on the Church, #42). See CELIBACY; CHASTITY.

VIRTUE

A good habit that enables a person to act according to right reason enlightened by faith and to do so with relative ease and with perseverance despite obstacles. The Christian tradition distinguishes especially between theological virtues and moral virtues. Theological virtues are powers infused by God with sanctifying grace, enabling the person to act on a supernatural level; they are faith, hope, and charity. The moral virtues are powers which are acquired by repeated human acts aided by the grace of God; there are many moral virtues, but the chief ones are prudence, justice, fortitude, and temperance. See THEOLOGICAL VIRTUES; FAITH; HOPE; CHARITY; PRUDENCE; JUSTICE; FORTITUDE; TEMPERANCE.

VOCATION

In a general sense, a call from God to salvation and holiness; thus, Vatican II speaks of the universal call (vocation) to holiness for all members of the Church. In a specific sense, a call to a particular way of life in the Church: to priesthood, religious life (as a priest, Sister, or Brother), Christian marriage, or the single life in the world.

VOW

As defined in the Code of Canon Law, ''A vow is a deliberate and free promise made to God concerning a possible and better good which must be fulfilled by reason of the virtue of religion'' (Canon 1191, §1). A vow is public if it is accepted in the name of the Church by a legitimate superior; otherwise, it is private. A vow is solemn if it is recognized as such by the Church; otherwise it is simple.

W

WAGE, JUST

According to Catholic social teaching, the matter of the just wage is one of the most important elements in the relationship between employer and employee. The most recent expression of this teaching is found in Pope John Paul II's encyclical entitled *On Human Work* (*Laborem Exercens*): "The key problem of social ethics in this case is that of remuneration for work done. In the context of the present there is no more important way of securing a just relationship between the worker and the employer than that constituted by remuneration for work" (#19). It is true that many complex questions arise about the working out of this moral obligation, but the moral teaching of the Church insists on several basic principles, among which are the following:

• The minimum just wage should be determined by the very reason why a person works — namely, to earn a livelihood.
• The just wage must take into consideration the requirements of the family. In the words of Pope John Paul II: "Just remuneration for the work of an adult who is responsible for a family means remuneration which will suffice for establishing and properly maintaining a family and providing security for its future" (#19).
• Women employees have a right to receive equal wages for equal work. See SOCIAL JUSTICE.

WAKE

This term describes the custom of remaining awake and on watch with a deceased person; it is usually a period of one or two days before the funeral when mourners may pay their respects to the deceased and offer their condolences to the bereaved. According to Catholic custom, the wake should also be a time of prayer for the repose of the soul of the deceased and for strength and courage on the part of the bereaved. It is customary in the United States to have a liturgical wake service (a "vigil for the deceased") and/or the praying of the rosary. See FUNERAL RITES.

WAR, MORALITY OF

In view of the fact that war involves many evils, including the maiming and killing of other human beings, the question about its morality arose early in the Christian community: Is it possible to justify war from a Christian viewpoint? The answer to this question gradually developed into what is commonly called "the just war theory." Briefly, this theory held that four conditions were necessary for a war to be just: (1) a war must be declared by lawful authority; (2) there must be a just cause, a serious grievance, for going to war; (3) there must be a right intention, such as true self-defense, not mere vengeance; (4) there must be a right use of means, that is, the war itself must be carried out in a moral manner. In modern times, Pope Pius XII (who was pope during the Second World War) frequently turned his attention to this just war theory. His views were adopted and expressed by Vatican Council II in what might be called an updated version of the just war theory. The following points are emphasized: (1) the only "just cause" for modern war would be as a means of self-defense against a very grave injustice that touches a free community of people, and provided that this injustice cannot be halted by any other means; (2) the "right use of means" demands that all weapons be subject to moral control, that indiscriminate destruction of whole cities or areas is morally wrong, that the rights of the innocent and noncombatants must be carefully safeguarded.

In the nuclear age, the question arises: Can this updated just war theory be applied to nuclear war? There are many people who believe that the just war theory cannot be applied to nuclear war; the moral safeguards simply cannot be observed. There are others, however, who maintain that even nuclear war may be conducted in a moral manner. In May 1983 the American Catholic bishops issued a comprehensive pastoral letter on peace and war, *The Challenge of Peace: God's Promise and Our Response*. The letter acknowledges the diversity of opinion among people of good will on the morality of using nuclear weapons in any form, but they insist that, if nuclear weapons may be used at all, they may be used only after they have been used against our country or our allies, and, even then, only in an extremely limited, discriminatory manner against military targets. The bishops seriously challenge the assumption that nuclear war can in fact be limited in this way. Moreover, they insist that every effort must be made to reduce and limit the arms race, that deterrence must not be seen as an end in itself but only as a temporary justification on the way toward a progressive disarmament.

WAY OF THE CROSS
A popular devotion (also called Stations of the Cross) in honor of the Passion and death of Christ; it consists of meditating on 14 "stations" or "stages" in the Passion of Christ, such as his condemnation by Pilate, his scourging, and the like. The stations are wooden crosses and may be attached to the walls of a church or oratory or erected outdoors. The stations must be lawfully erected and blessed by one having authority to do so.

WISDOM
One of the gifts of the Holy Spirit that enables a person to have a true appreciation (or taste) for the things of God and to have right judgment in discerning and choosing what is true and good.

WISDOM BOOKS
This term refers to certain books of the Bible: namely, the books of Job, Psalms, Proverbs, Ecclesiastes, Song of Songs, Wisdom, and Sirach. These books belong to what is often called "the wisdom literature" of the Bible. Their purpose is to instruct one on understanding and solving the vital questions of human life, such as the search for happiness, the problem of evil, the distinction between good and evil in human life, the meaning of death and what lies beyond. Such wisdom is a gift of Yahweh and should be prayed for.

WITNESS
As a Christian idea, this word means that the believer gives testimony to his or her faith in Jesus Christ and his Gospel in all of his or her thoughts, words, and deeds, even at the cost of personal sacrifice or hostility on the part of others.

WORD OF GOD

An expression used to describe several different realities: notably, Jesus Christ as the Word of God (see John 1:1,14); and the Bible as containing "the Word of God in the words of men."

WORK

Catholic social teaching has long emphasized that human work or labor, whether of a physical or mental nature, is of great importance to human dignity and to Christian spirituality. This teaching was expressed most recently in the encyclical of Pope John Paul II, *On Human Work* (*Laborem Exercens*): "Work is not only good in the sense that it is something to enjoy; it is also good in the sense of being something worthy, that is to say, something that corresponds to man's dignity, that expresses his dignity and increases it. If one wishes to define more clearly the ethical meaning of work, it is this truth that one must particularly keep in mind. Work is a good thing for man — a good thing for his humanity — because through work man not only transforms nature, adapting it to his own needs, but he also achieves fulfillment as a human being and indeed becomes 'more a human being' " (#9).

WORSHIP

See ADORATION.

X, Y, Z

YAHWEH

A Hebrew name for God meaning, approximately, "I am who
am" (see Exodus 3:13-14); it especially designates God as
Creator of the universe and the Source of all life. Sometimes
translated into English as *Jehovah*. See GOD.

YEAR, LITURGICAL

The liturgical year, in the words of Vatican II, "unfolds the whole
mystery of Christ." The liturgical year begins with the first
Sunday of Advent, a season of approximately four weeks, with
emphasis on the coming of Christ both at the end of time and into
human history. The Christmas season, celebrating the Incarnation of Jesus Christ, begins with the vigil of Christmas and
lasts until the Sunday after January 6. The period between the
end of the Christmas season and the beginning of Lent belongs to
the Ordinary Time of the year. The season of Lent, with special
emphasis on conversion and penance, begins on Ash Wednesday
and lasts until the Mass of the Lord's Supper on Holy Thursday.
The Easter Triduum begins with evening Mass of the Lord's
Supper on Holy Thursday and ends with evening prayer on Easter
Sunday. The Easter season lasts from Easter until Pentecost, a
period of 50 days, with emphasis on our sharing in the Resurrection of Christ. Ordinary Time resumes on the Monday after
Pentecost and continues until the beginning of Advent, com-
prising 33 or 34 weeks. Throughout the liturgical year, "holy
Church honors with special love the Blessed Mary, Mother of
God" (for example, on December 8, feast of the Immaculate
Conception), and includes "days devoted to the memory of the
martyrs and other saints." See ADVENT; EASTER; LENT.

ZECHARIAH, BOOK OF

One of the Prophetic Books of the Old Testament; written in 520 B.C., it is noteworthy especially for its many prophecies concerning the Messiah and the messianic kingdom.

ZEPHANIAH, BOOK OF

One of the Prophetic Books of the Old Testament; written in the second half of the seventh century before Christ, it contains strong prophecies of punishment for Jerusalem and its people because of their idolatry and superstition; it also predicts, however, that a holy remnant of the people will be spared.

SUGGESTED READING

The following encyclopedias and dictionaries are available from their respective publishers.

New Catholic Encyclopedia. McGraw-Hill, 1967. This work (in 18 volumes) is the most complete treatment of the Catholic Church available in English.

Broderick, Robert C. *The Catholic Encyclopedia.* Thomas Nelson, 1976. A one-volume work which includes in its definitions and descriptions many extended quotes from the documents of Vatican II.

Foy, Felician A., O.F.M., ed. *1985 Catholic Almanac.* Our Sunday Visitor Press, 1985. An extremely valuable source of information on almost every aspect of the Catholic Church in the United States.

Hardon, John A., S.J., *Modern Catholic Dictionary.* Doubleday, 1980. A solid treatment of Catholic topics presented in a straightforward, nontechnical way.

McKenzie, John L. *Dictionary of the Bible.* Macmillan, 1965. A comprehensive dictionary of the people, places, and beliefs in the Bible.

Rahner, Karl, and Herbert Vorgrimler. *Dictionary of Theology.* Crossroad, 1981. Somewhat technical discussions of Catholic beliefs; for the serious student of Catholic theology.

BOOKS BY THE SAME AUTHOR

FOLLOWING CHRIST
A Handbook of Catholic Moral Teaching
$3.95

CATHOLIC BELIEFS, LAWS, PRACTICES
26 Questions and Answers
$1.95

CHOOSING VIRTUE IN A CHANGING WORLD
A New Look at the Seven Deadly Sins
$2.95

DAY BY DAY THROUGH LENT
Reflections, Prayers, Practices
$3.95

DAY BY DAY THROUGH ADVENT
Reflections, Prayers, Practices
$2.95

PAMPHLETS BY THE SAME AUTHOR
75¢

Infant Baptism
New Questions, New Answers

So You're Getting Married

The Commandments of the Church

Mini-Meditations for Lent

When We Meet Eternity

OTHER HELPFUL PUBLICATIONS FROM LIGUORI

THE ILLUSTRATED CATECHISM
Catholic Belief in Words and Pictures

An important review/reference book for every Catholic home! Over 250 illustrations and a question-and-answer format that includes:

The Christian Vision — Shows how Jesus revealed himself as Redeemer.

The Church — Shows how the Church is a hierarchical community established by Jesus to be an infallible sign of his presence in the world.

The Sacraments — Presents the seven signs of Christ's continuing activity in his Church.

The Dignity of the Christian — Shows how to work for the dignity of all men in the kingdom of God.

Prayer — Shows how the Holy Spirit leads the Christian to the Father through Jesus.

Supplement —Provides practical help for the everyday Catholic in the twentieth century.

THE ILLUSTRATED CATECHISM uses the latest educational methods to combine the wisdom of the great theologians of the past with the teachings of present-day scholars — to introduce today's generations to the teachings of the Catholic Church. $5.95

Leader's Guide available — $4.95